Praise for *Control Alt Achieve*

Reading this book is like sitting in on a presentation from one of educational technology's best presenters from your couch and in your pajamas. Eric's writing reminds me of his sessions: comfortable and accessible for new tech users while still valuable for experienced users.

—Jake Miller, @JakeMillerTech, host of the Educational Duct Tape Podcast

Ready to kick things up a notch with technology in your classroom? Eric has got your back! Put your students in the driver's seat to take CONTROL of their learning. In this book, you will find exciting, ALTernative ways to integrate technology and engage students. Better yet, Eric will walk you through not only how to enhance the learning but to also cultivate student ACHIEVEment.

—Kasey Bell, international speaker, author, and digital learning coach at ShakeUpLearning.com

Eric Curts is a pedagogy + technology WIZARD! You won't find any "check the box" or digital bubble sheets in *Control Alt Achieve*. I'm so excited to know that his amazing Google wizardry and approach to lesson design are being unleashed on educators in this amazing collection of creativity and fun.

—Jon Corippo, author, *The Eduprotocol Field Guide* and *The Eduprotocol Field Guide Book 2*

Eric's blog has long been one of the best resources for inspiring ideas and easy-to-follow lessons. Finally, he is putting his genius into a book that is easy to read and even easier to follow. It will motivate teachers with ideas on how to empower teaching and learning in the classroom. You won't be disappointed by this book, and one copy should be on the desk of every educator hoping to infuse their classrooms with meaningful technology-integration ideas.

—Holly Clark, Author, *The Google Infused Classroom*

I have been a big fan of Eric's website for some time and am thrilled he has finally released this resource for educators with tips and activities for all subject areas and grades. Eric includes clear, step-by-step instructions for activities that will spark creativity and engage students of every age. Whether you are new to teaching (or Google) or a veteran, Eric will take you outside the box to look at Google apps in a whole new way. Moreover, it is fun to read! Eric's comical, down-to-earth voice is present on every page. So grab your computer and a beverage, sit down, and get ready to find a gold mine of Google activities to use in your practice tomorrow.

—Jen Giffen, @VirtualGiff, teacher, librarian, Richmond Hill, ON, Canada, cohost of Shukes and Giff the Podcast

Eric Curts shares his endless creativity and wisdom in each chapter of *Control Alt Achieve*. This book is overflowing with phenomenal ideas for incorporating technology into any classroom. Each chapter is packed with Google Docs, Slides, Drawings, and Sheets projects for all grades and technology experience levels!

—Mari Venturino, middle school science teacher, San Diego, CA

Eric Curts knows his stuff! He is my go-to when it comes to bringing new technologies into the classroom.

—Donnie Piercey, fifth grade teacher

Control Alt Achieve provides both practical and pedagogical strategies that go way beyond simple technology integration. This is a great handbook for any teacher that is looking to go beyond the how-to and shift toward a learning transformation.

—Ken Shelton, Kennethshelton.net

In *Control Alt Achieve*, educational-technology guru Eric Curts provides teachers with excellent and practical ideas for using familiar Google tools, including Docs, Slides, Drawings, and Sheets, in new ways to engage learners. These reboots offer a fresh take for teachers looking to design learning experiences for their students that use technology in meaningful ways. I love the "poke a stick at it" suggestion for teachers when we aren't sure exactly what a feature actually does. Try it and see what happens! You'll definitely learn something new from *Control Alt Achieve*!

—**Bethany Petty,** @Bethany_Petty, teacher, author, and speaker

Eric takes you beyond the traditional uses of a tool to give you tangible innovation so you can take your teaching with technology to the next level.

—**Alice Keeler,** @alicekeeler, teacher, edtech expert, Google Certified Innovator

In this book, Eric has created a powerful method to meaningfully integrate technology into teaching and learning. His unique way of crafting technology-rich experiences will allow anyone from a novice techie to an edtech expert the ability to control, alt, achieve!

—**Michael Cohen,** the Tech Rabbi, creativity instigator and author of *Educated By Design*

Eric Curts has long been one of my #edtech heroes. His ability to not only make it easy for educators to leverage tools to improve student creativity and learning but to showcase innovative practices that engage and excite students has often been something I have sought to emulate. In *Control Alt Achieve* we get to see Eric's talents on full display with a veritable greatest hits of activities that contains easy-to-follow instructions for educators to implement while being inventive enough to capture the imagination of every student! If you are looking for a book to help take your classroom up to the next level, look no further. *Control Alt Achieve* is here to lead the way!

—**Jesse Lubinsky,** chief learning officer, Ready Learner One, LLC

Eric Curts is the Google guru you've been looking for. If you want to level up your Google skills, teach engaging Googley activities, and smile the whole way, you're going to LOVE this book.

—**Matt Miller,** author of *Ditch That Textbook*

Control Alt Achieve

Published by Dave Burgess Consulting, Inc.
San Diego, CA
DaveBurgessConsulting.com

Library of Congress Control Number: 2020936167
Paperback ISBN: 978-1-951600-26-6
E-book ISBN: 978-1-951600-27-3

Cover and interior design by Liz Schreiter

Dedicated to my daughter, Chrissee. I have spent my entire life creating things, but no matter what I do, you will always be the greatest thing I have ever made. I am so proud to be your dad. Love you always!

CONTENTS

Introduction xi

SECTION 1: REBOOTING GOOGLE DOCS

1: Checking Word Count 2

2: Highlighting to Solve Story Problems 4

3: Blackout Highlighting 6

4: Blackout Poetry 8

5: Inserting Google Drawings 11

6: Emoji Learning Activities. 14

7: Creating a Story with Branching Paths 20

8: Rebooting You: Poke a Stick at It 23

SECTION 2: REBOOTING GOOGLE SLIDES

9: Collabordependent Writing. 28

10: Drag-and-Drop Manipulative Activities. 32

11: Video Mash-Ups. 35

12: Stop-Motion Animation. 39

13: Creating E-Books and Comic Strips 42

14: Interactive Slides with Pear Deck Add-On. 45

15: Nonlinear Slides for Stories, Quizzes, and More 49

16: Flash Cards for Randomized Quizzing. 52

17: Rebooting You: The Big Blank Wall 56

SECTION 3: REBOOTING GOOGLE DRAWINGS

18: Desktop Publishing 60

19: Motivational Posters 64

20: Memes. 66

21: Greeting Cards 68

22: Background-Removal Activities 70

23: Graphic Organizers 72

24: Pattern-Block Activities. 76

25: Math Activities 78

26: Story Cubes. 81

27: Googlink Interactive Images. 83

28: Rebooting You: The Bionic Educator 87

SECTION 4: REBOOTING GOOGLE SHEETS

29: Interactive Learning Databases 90

30: Self-Checking Assessments 95

31: Pixel Art Activities. 98

32: Mondrian Art Activity. 101

33: Random Writing Prompt Generator 104

34: Emoji Writing Prompt Generator 106

35: Educational Games and Activities with Flippity. 108

36: Rebooting You: KISS and Tech Up 112

Acknowledgments 115

About the Author 117

INTRODUCTION

How many uses can you think of for a screwdriver? Take a minute and see what you come up with.

Of course, there is the original use, as evident in the name: to drive screws into wood or such. As any poor college student or desperate homeowner can testify, though, a screwdriver can be a very versatile tool. I have personally used one to:

- Open an envelope
- Stir paint
- Weed my flower beds
- Pry open a door
- Clean out gutters
- Chisel the Ohio winter ice
- Scratch that itch on my back I can't reach
- Clean the dog doo out of my shoe treads
- And even serve as a microphone when lip-syncing (after cleaning it, of course)

Just like a screwdriver, technology tools can also be used in a wide variety of ways beyond their original purposes. For example:

- Google Docs is a word processor, but it can do more than just process words. Docs can be used to create blackout poetry and emoji stories.
- Sure, Google Slides can make slideshows, but students can also use it to make stop-motion animation and comic strips, or play various learning games (such as *Jeopardy!*).
- Google Sheets is a great spreadsheet tool for crunching numbers, but it can also allow students to create online games, pixel art, and learning databases.

- Google Drawings is great for making diagrams, but can also be used for interactive posters, magnetic poetry, and educational math manipulatives.

It is my passion to find creative ways to use technology in education. I love looking at a tool from a 90-degree angle and thinking of how, moving beyond its original purpose, students can use it to create and learn.

This perspective comes in part from working in settings where budgets are tight and teachers need to make the most of limited resources. When I worked for North Canton City Schools in Ohio, I served as a math teacher and then as a technology integrationist. North Canton was long known as the "Home of Hoover Appliances," and for years the local factory provided wonderful financial support for the school system. When Hoover left the city, though, so did the company's tax dollars, and suddenly we were struggling to provide technology for our students and staff.

That's when I discovered G Suite for Education. With Google's free tools we were able to find ways to extend learning opportunities for our students at no cost.

A second reason I have embraced nontraditional uses of technology is that this approach encourages us to focus on learning, not the tool. There are loads of specialized apps and gadgets—and that is wonderful—but we can't think of the tool as an end in itself. Instead, we need to ask:

- What can students create with this tool?
- How can this tool help students work together?
- How can students use this tool to express what they have learned?

It is this passion that led me to launch my blog, *Control Alt Achieve,* where I share creative ways to reboot our classrooms with technology. And now it has led to this book—where you will find loads of practical, ready-to-use ideas and projects for G Suite and other tech tools.

I hope you will also be inspired to look at technology in a new way. If you thought a screwdriver was useful, just think how many ways we can use technology for teaching and learning!

G Suite provides many benefits: anywhere/anytime access, autosave, voice typing, the Explore tool, collaboration features, and more. Many sample activities I identify in the book have traditionally been done using paper, markers, and highlighters—but there are great benefits to doing these activities in G Suite. For example:

- There's no need to use multiple copies of resources such as magazines or newspaper articles.
- There's no waste, since there is nothing physical to be thrown away when done.
- It's easy to make changes to projects and undo mistakes.
- It's easy for students to share their work with others.
- It's easy to display final products online or projected for the class to see and discuss.

Many of these activities call for you to share a project that you have created or a template I have provided with your class. There are two ways to do this. First, you could push out a copy to each student through Google Classroom.

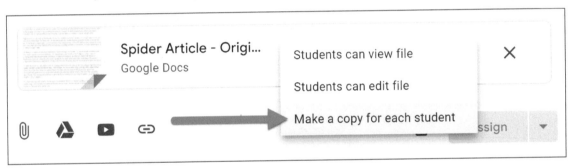

- Go to Google Classroom.
- Click the button to **Create assignment**.
- Fill in the details for the assignment.
- Click the **Google Drive icon** and choose the Google Doc with the article text.
- From the drop-down menu to the right, choose **Make a copy for each student**.
- Finally, click **Assign**, and each student will get their own copy of the Google Doc to work on.

If you are not using Google Classroom, a second option would be to share the Google Doc with your students with *view-only rights*.

- Click the big blue **Share button** in the top right corner of the Google Doc.
- When the **Share with others** window opens, click **Get shareable link** in the top right corner.
- Select **Anyone with the link can view** from the drop-down menu.
- This will generate a link that will allow others to view the document. Provide this link to your students through email, on your class website, or with a shortened URL.
- When students open the shared Doc, they can make their own copy by clicking **File** and then **Make a copy**.

Once students have finished these activities, it is easy for them to share their final projects. Students can share their work in several ways, as reviewed here:

- With Google Classroom, the end product can be turned in through the assignment page.
- The project can be shared with others by using the **Share** button in the top corner—students can share with specific people or share via a link.
- The project can also be downloaded in PDF format. Students simply click **File,** then **Download as,** and then **PDF Document**.
- Students can also print out their projects.
- The link or downloaded project can be shared with others in many ways:
    - Link it on the class website.
    - Share it on social media such as Twitter or Facebook.
    - Send it in an email to others.
    - Make a QR code from it.
    - Use a URL shortener such as bit.ly or tiny.cc to make a shorter, easier-to-share version of the link (great for placement in printed materials such as newsletters).

RESOURCES

Throughout this book many templates, resources, and websites will be referenced. Links to all of these can be found on my blog at the "Book Links" page associated with this book at: **www.controlaltachieve.com/booklinks**.

REBOOTING GOOGLE DOCS

1: CHECKING WORD COUNT

Certainly one of our goals as educators is for our students to write more. Writing more is not necessarily the same thing as writing more words, though—in fact, there are several benefits to having our students write fewer words.

It is a valuable way for students to distill their ideas, selecting just the most important, relevant, clear, and concise words. Putting limits on the number of words or characters our students can use forces them to:

- Summarize key points
- Select what is most important
- Choose words that best convey their meaning
- Restate concepts
- Avoid unnecessary filler and fluff

In this chapter, we will look at how students can use the **Word Count tool** in Google Docs to easily check how many words and/or characters they have written. This is practical for writing activities where you specifically limit the length of students' writing. It is also helpful for you as a teacher when it comes time to evaluate their writing, to quickly verify the word count.

When it comes to word count, I will try to keep it short. As Shakespeare wrote, "Brevity is the soul of wit."

CHOOSE YOUR WORD LIMIT AND TOPIC

First, you will want to decide *what limit to give your students* for their writing. You might decide to limit them to a certain number of words or a specific number of characters.

Your students will have to write something that fits within those restrictions. What they write might be:

- A summary of a story they are reading
- The main point of an article
- A description of a character
- A clear statement of an argument
- A new title for a story, book, play, or movie
- The dust-jacket blurb for a book
- The Netflix description for a movie
- A personal definition for a vocabulary word
- An ELI5 (that stands for "Explain Like I'm Five") from science, math, social studies, et cetera
- A Tweet summarizing their thoughts on an article, chapter, book, concepts, et cetera

The point is that students will need to *concentrate their ideas* into a smaller number of words, which forces them to really consider what is most important and how to communicate that clearly.

✏ Use the Word Count Tool

Now that you have the assignment and the limit, it is time for the students to write. As they write, though, they will need to keep checking how many words or characters they have used, depending on the limit set. They can do this easily with the Word Count tool built into Google Docs.

To walk through it:

- **Select the text** you have typed. If there is other text in the document, be sure to just select the portion you wrote and want to get the word count for.

Novel Summary Assignment

Using a maximum of 140 characters, write a summary of the novel you read.

Watership Down is the story of a group of rabbits searching for a new home. Led by Hazel, the rabbits face many obstacles and threats from humans and other animals. In the end they find and defend a new home.

- Next, click **Tools** in the top menu bar and select **Word count** from the drop-down menu.
- You will now see a pop-up window with the statistics.
- **Words** indicates the number of words selected, of the total number of words in the document.
- **Characters** shows the number of characters selected, of the total number of characters in the document.
- Whether counting words or characters, you will want to take note of the first number, since that will be the count from the text you have written and selected.
- Click **Close** when you are done.

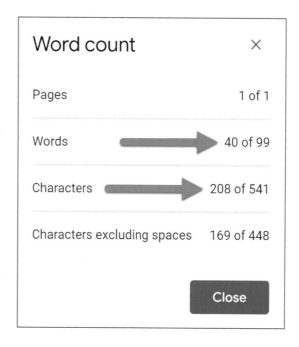

As needed, students can now edit what they have written. They may need to reduce the number of words or characters by deleting content, rewriting, or summarizing. Or they may still have some room to expand a bit and can add more details.

Throughout the process, students should keep using the Word Count tool to see what impact their changes have had, until they are within the limits you have set.

2: HIGHLIGHTING TO SOLVE STORY PROBLEMS

If Bob leaves at noon on a westbound train traveling 60 miles per hour, and Mary leaves at 1 p.m. on an eastbound train traveling 70 miles per hour, how many minutes will it take before you suffer a math-induced panic attack?

If solving story problems brings back grade-school anxiety, you are not alone. Many students struggle with word problems. Such problems are more challenging because they require higher-level skills in Bloom's taxonomy, such as evaluating, analyzing, and creating. We may feel comfortable (relatively speaking) with math when simply given an expression to evaluate, but it can be much more difficult to decide what is important, determine relationships, see what is missing, and construct a plan for a solution when we are confronted with a story problem.

One option for helping students break down a story problem is to use **highlighting** in Google Docs. Ordinarily we may think of highlighting as just a tool for language arts, but reading is a skill that applies across all areas of the curriculum. Highlighting can be just as useful for story problems as it is for storybooks. As a class you can assign meaning to colors and then highlight text in your document accordingly. This color-coding can be used to identify parts of speech, main ideas and their supporting details, or the elements of a math story problem.

THE PROBLEM

First things first, we need a problem to solve. For this example we will go with something basic to emphasize how the highlighting tool can be used.

> Mason has 12 Pokémon cards, while his brother Carter has 7 cards and his other brother Grant has 9 cards. If Mason decides to share his cards equally between himself and his two brothers, how many total cards will Grant end up with?

DEVELOP A COLOR CODE

An essential part of solving a story problem is reading through the text to identify the values given, the operations, the question being asked, and any unnecessary information. One way to do this is by highlighting the text in the story problem to call out these different parts.

For example, the following colors could be used for the different parts of a story problem:

- **Light blue** = Given values. These are the numbers and quantities we will be working with in the problem.
- **Light red** = Operations. These are the words that indicate mathematical operations, such as "more than" for addition or "shared between" for division.
- **Light green** = Question to answer. This is the part of the problem that indicates what we are trying to find, calculate, or determine.
- **Light gray** = Unrelated information. These are distractions that provide us with information we can ignore.

✎ HIGHLIGHT THE TEXT

Using the established color code, students can read through the story problem and highlight the text with the appropriate colors. To do this:

- **Select** the text you want to highlight.
- Click the **Highlight color** button in the top toolbar.
- Select the **color** you'd like to use.
- The selected text will be highlighted.
- Repeat this process for other text throughout the document as needed.

For our example we might end up with something like this:

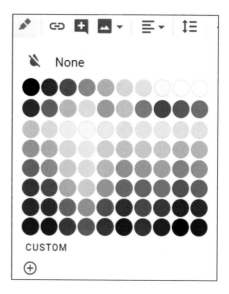

Sample Math Problem

Mason has 12 Pokemon cards, while his brother Carter has 7 cards and his other brother Grant has 9 cards. If Mason decided to share his cards between himself and his two brothers, how many total cards would Grant end up with?

✎ BENEFITS

Using these highlighting colors can be helpful in several ways:

- It helps the student process the story problem, break it down into its parts, and identify the key information.
- It helps the student eliminate extra, unnecessary information that is not really part of the problem.
- It can allow groups of students, or the entire class, to compare how they colored the problem and come to an agreement on how to solve the problem.
- It can help you as the teacher to identify where a student may have misconceptions in solving the problem.

By the way, did you get "13 cards" for the answer to the story problem? Good job!

3: BLACKOUT HIGHLIGHTING

Key skills for literacy are reading comprehension, identifying main ideas, and summarization. Many excellent practices can help students develop these abilities.

A few years ago, I came across a creative technique called text-reduction strategy. I liked the idea but also felt it could be made even better with a Google Docs technology twist. The original idea goes like this:

- Students are given a magazine article and a black marker.
- They are instructed to read the article and decide what text is critical to the main point of the article and what text is not.
- Next, they use the marker to black out any text that is not critical, leaving behind just the main ideas.

The benefit of this activity is that students do not have to come up with their own words to summarize the article. Instead, all the words are already there, and students are using their critical thinking skills to determine what is most important. This can be a helpful stepping-stone toward improving their reading comprehension while working toward better summarization skills.

As much as I loved the idea, I thought it would be great to take it a step further and use technology rather than physical paper magazines and black markers. This activity works great in Google Docs, and even picks up a few added benefits by going digital:

- No need for physical magazines, news articles, or markers
- Easy to make changes, unlike when using a permanent marker
- Ability to use assistive tech during the project, such as speech-to-text.
- Many options for sharing and comparing student work
- No waste to throw away when done

FIND AN ARTICLE

First, you will need an article for your students to read. There are many excellent websites that provide current-event and high-interest articles for students. Some are specific to certain grade levels, while others provide multiple versions of their articles at different Lexile levels so that students of all ages can engage with the writing. A few great sites to consider for articles include:

- Newsela: newsela.com
- TweenTribune: tweentribune.com
- Wonderopolis: wonderopolis.org
- DOGOnews: dogonews.com
- Here There Everywhere: htekidsnews.com
- Youngzine: youngzine.org
- Scholastic News: magazines.scholastic.com
- National Geographic Kids: kids.nationalgeographic.com/explore
- Science News for Students: sciencenewsforstudents.org

PUT THE ARTICLE IN GOOGLE DOCS

For this step, you will need to copy and paste the text of an article into a Google Doc. If the article is on a web page that also has lots of other text, comments, or sidebar information, it might be difficult to select just the text from the article itself. Normally when you copy and paste text from a website into a Doc, it brings with it whatever formatting the text had, such as font, color, and size. For this "blackout" activity, it is best for the text to be as plain and simple as possible, with no extra formatting at all. Thankfully, there is an easy way to paste just the copied text, with no formatting:

- Select the text, **B** on the selected text, then choose **Copy**.
- Or select the text and press **Ctrl** and **Shift** and **C.**
- Next, click inside the Google Doc.
- Press **Ctrl** and **Shift** and **V.**
- Or click **Edit** and **Paste without formatting**.
- Or right-click and choose **Paste without formatting**.
- The copied text will now be pasted into the Google Doc as plain text with no special formatting.

STUDENTS "BLACK OUT" THE ARTICLE

Once you have shared the document with your students (as outlined in the Introduction), they can do the "blackout" activity. They need to read the article and decide which text is critical to the main point and which text is not. Their goal is to black out any text that is not critical, leaving behind just the main ideas. This can be done by using the built-in **highlighter tool** as described in the previous chapter, but choosing black for the color.

To save some time, you can also use the **Paint format tool** to quickly apply the black highlighting to other sections of text (special thanks to Amy Farris for this great tip!):

- First, select some text that is already highlighted black.
- Next, double-click on the **Paint format** button on the top menu bar. Double-clicking will "lock in" the copied formatting.
- Simply select any other text in the document and the black highlighting will automatically be applied to it.
- When done, just click the **Paint format** button again to turn it off.

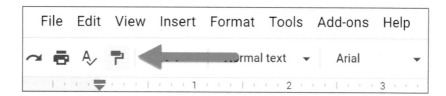

If you think you made a mistake and want to remove the black out from some text, you can do that:

- First, click and drag your mouse to select the blacked-out text.
- When you do this, the black highlighting will turn slightly lighter, allowing you to read the blacked-out text.
- If you find some text you want to remove the black out from, select just that text.
- Then, click the **Text color** button in the top toolbar.

- Click the **Highlight** option in the drop-down menu.
- Click the **None** option.
- The black highlighting will be removed from that text, and it will reappear.

When the student is finished, the Google Doc will have blacked-out text for a large amount of the content, leaving just the most important information visible. This may be just topic sentences, key phrases, et cetera.

The next time you shriek at the sight of a spider, be aware that the arachnid can hear you loud and clear, from as far as away as 10 feet! The surprising discovery by Cornell University researchers adds to the already impressive list of arachnid attributes that includes superior vision and ability to weave intricate webs.

▮▮▮▮▮▮▮▮▮▮▮▮▮▮ the arachnid can hear you loud and clear, from as far as away as 10 feet! ▮▮▮▮▮ discovery by Cornell University researchers ▮▮▮▮▮ ▮▮▮▮▮▮▮▮▮▮▮▮▮▮▮

At this stage, the students can share their final products with their teacher or with other students. Blackout articles from different students could be compared to see what different classmates thought was most important.

RESOURCES

You can access the following digital resources for this project via the "Book Links" page of my blog:

- Links to websites with articles for students
- Google Doc with an original article about spiders
- Version of article with blacked-out text

4: BLACKOUT POETRY

Another fun way to use blackout with Docs and engage students in poetry is by having them create blackout poems. Start by giving the student a page of text, as described below. The student then blacks out all of the text except for the words they want to leave behind to form a poem. This can be helpful for students struggling to write a poem, since they do not need to come up with any words of their own, but instead are working within a set of available words that appear in a particular order. It can also be fun to see the variety of poems students create by starting with the same original text. The final poems can be compared to see if similar themes emerge, or to note the creation of completely different moods and ideas.

Often this activity is done with paper and big black markers, but blackout poetry works great in a digital format. Using Google Docs and a few simple tricks, students can easily create and share poems.

PREPARE THE ORIGINAL TEXT IN GOOGLE DOCS

Blackout poetry is based on students removing words from a provided text, so you need to begin with the text they will work from. This could be text from a book, an article, a blog post, or another source. If you are looking for kid-friendly articles to start from, see the list of websites in the previous section or find the links on the "Book Links" page of my blog.

Also, if you would like the student poems to have a particular theme, you can always search for articles that have a specific keyword in them, such as *love, family, war,* or *prejudice.* For my simple example I searched for an article related to trees and came across an article from DOGOnews, which you can find on the "Book Links" page.

Once you have the text, **copy and paste it into a Google Doc.** However, it is best for the text to be as *plain and simple as possible* with no extra formatting at all. As mentioned in the previous section, you can **Paste without formatting** so that the copied text will be pasted into the Google Doc as plain text with no special formatting.

Once you have the text in the Google Doc, you may want to reformat it a bit so it fits nicely on one page. For example:

- Change the font size.
- Delete some of the text if it is too long.
- Change the page to landscape format if you find that looks better for creating a poem (click **File,** then **Page setup** and click the radio button next to **Landscape**).

When the original text is all ready, simply provide it to your students.

CHANGE THE PAGE BACKGROUND TO A TEMPORARY COLOR

Now that the students have the Google Doc with the source text, they can begin to make their blackout poem. Typically, the students will only keep a small portion of the words for their final poem, blacking out most of the words. A few tricks can make the process much faster for the students. The first step will be to temporarily make the page background color something other than white or black.

To do this, the student should:

- Click **File** in the top menu bar.
- Choose **Page setup** from the drop-down menu.
- Click the **Page color** option.
- From the pop-up menu, **choose a color** other than white or black, such as gray.
- Click **OK** to make the color change.

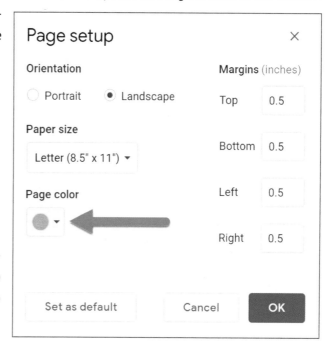

Now the entire page will have a gray background (or whatever color you chose). This will make it much easier to do the next step, which is highlighting the words we want to keep in the poem.

HIGHLIGHT THE CHOSEN WORDS WITH WHITE

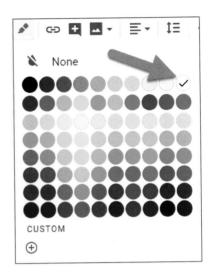

Next, students can begin choosing the words they want to keep to make their poems. They should read through the text looking for key words and ideas they want to use. When they have found some words they want to keep, students should select those words, click **Highlight color** in the top toolbar, and choose white for the color. This will allow their chosen words to stand out now, and to remain visible later when the blackout is done.

Students can repeat this process with the rest of the words they want to save. However, to save some time, they can also use the **Paint format tool** to quickly apply the white highlighting to other words, as described in the previous chapter.

When all this is done, the poem words should all be highlighted in white. With one more simple step, students can black out everything else, leaving just the poem they created.

a sliver off one of the trees that includes the bud, I insert it into a like-size incision in the working tree, tape it, let it sit and heal in all winter, then I prune it back and hope that it grows." The end result is a tree that is everything the professor could have hoped for and more. During the spring, when the various grafted parts yield a bouquet of crimson, pink, purple and white blooms, it is a work of art. In the summer, as the flowers transform into gorgeous, rarely seen stone fruits, the tree becomes a conservation project. What makes the

CHANGE THE PAGE BACKGROUND TO BLACK

For the final step in making the poem, students will want to change the page background color to black. They should follow the same Page color directions as before, but choose black as the color this time. Because all the text is black, by making the page background black, all the text will seem to disappear except the words that were previously highlighted with a white background. This is a quick and simple way to black out all of the unused text without the need to go through and black out each word individually. When this is done, the entire page will be black except for the words students originally highlighted with a white background.

Students can now share their poems with the class.

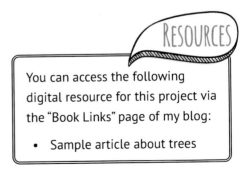

You can access the following digital resource for this project via the "Book Links" page of my blog:

- Sample article about trees

5: Inserting Google Drawings

"You can't do that in Google Docs!"

If you have ever made that claim, then you know the frustration of loving all the awesome things you can do in Docs, but still bumping up against limitations.

Sometimes we can extend the capabilities of Docs by installing add-ons or extensions. However, there is another powerful tool that's been sitting right there in the Docs menu all this time, which can provide you with loads of extra features that you may not have realized you had.

That tool is ... Google Drawings.

That's right. You can embed Google Drawings into your Doc right from the Insert menu. Being able to insert a live, editable Google Drawing into your document can let you do lots of things you normally cannot do in Google Docs. This can let you make your documents more interactive for students by adding multimedia, creating HyperDocs, and much more. There is a whole section in this book about creating different tools and activities in Drawings, so this chapter will focus on how to get those drawings into Docs and how to use the tools found in Docs to format your drawing for your document.

Add a Drawing

Many lessons benefit from having visual aids that help explain different concepts. Some lessons for which I have inserted Drawings are:

- Comparing and contrasting characters from a story
- Using a Frayer model to define a term from class, such as a landform a student is studying
- Matching letter sounds to images
- Putting in order the steps of a butterfly life cycle, or the parts of a story, or the path blood follows through the body, or the sentences in a paragraph
- Adding lines of symmetry to shapes
- Determining congruence of shapes by moving, rotating, and flipping them
- Sorting items by season, size, shape, color, et cetera

To teach my lesson on landforms, I was able to create a graphic organizer in Drawings and then insert it into my Doc. To do this:

- Open a **Google Doc** as usual.
- Click **Insert,** then **Drawing,** then **New**.
- This will open a pop-up window with the Google Drawing tools and canvas.
- You can now create your Google Drawing as usual (see Section 3 for many activities to create and detailed instructions on how to create them).
- When you are done, click **Save and close**.
- This will take the Drawing you have created and insert it into the Google Doc.

You can adjust the embedded Drawing in several ways:

- Click on the inserted Drawing to select it.
- Click and drag the Drawing to move it around the page.
- Change the size by clicking and dragging its **blue square handles.**
- Change the wrapping to **Wrap text** if you want text to wrap around the Drawing on all sides no matter where you drag it on the page.
- If you need to do any more editing in the Drawing, simply **double-click** on the embedded Drawing to reopen it in edit mode.

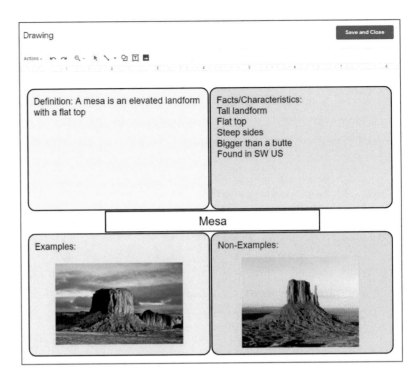

NOTE

If you share a Google Doc that has a Drawing embedded, the people you share it with can only view the Drawing, unless you give them edit rights to the Doc. If they have edit rights to the Doc, then they can also double-click on the Drawing to open and edit it.

✎ ADD A VIDEO

Google Docs does not currently have a way to easily add a videos to your document. So we have to get creative. One option is to use Google Drawings (with a little additional help from Google Slides). Here's how:

1. First, begin by **creating a slideshow** with Google Slides. You will use this only temporarily to copy the video you need, so you do not need to do anything fancy.
2. Once you have a blank Google Slides presentation, **insert a video** into one of the slides.
3. Click **Insert** in the top menu bar, then choose **Video** from the drop-down menu.
4. If the video is on YouTube, you can **search for the video** or **paste in the URL** for the video.
5. If the video is saved on your Google Drive, you can **search or browse through your Drive** to find it. Please note that if you're linking a video from your Google Drive, you'll need to share the video so that students can view it.
6. After you insert the video, you can choose to adjust the start and/or end time for the video if you do not want all of it to play by selecting **Video options** in the top toolbar.

Now that you have the video ready, you will copy and paste it into your Doc:

1. Open the **Google Doc** you want to add the video to.
2. Click **Insert** in the top menu bar, then choose **Drawing,** then **New**.
3. This will open a **blank Google Drawing canvas**.
4. If you have not already copied the video from your Google Slides, do that now by **selecting** the video and **copying** it.
5. In the blank Google Drawing canvas, **paste the copied video**.
6. You can **move** and **resize** the video as needed.
7. You can change text **wrapping** around the video as needed.
8. To play the video you simply need to double-click on the video in the Doc (which will open the Drawing window) and then double-click on the video again to start playing it.
9. When done, click **Save and close**.

The video will be embedded in the Google Drawing, which is now embedded in the Google Doc. Sort of like a technology turducken.

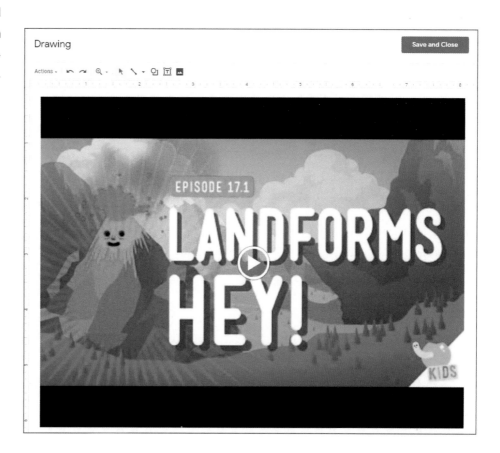

You can access the following digital resource via the "Book Links" page on my blog:

- A finished example of a HyperDoc called "Landforms"

6: EMOJI LEARNING ACTIVITIES

Emojis are a great tool to use in student learning activities, for many reasons:

- Since emojis are images, they can be used with students of any age, language, or reading ability.
- They can provide and represent a wide range of ideas, since each student will have their own interpretations of the pictures.
- Emojis are very popular with students, so they will likely have familiarity with the images.
- They are fun!

Thankfully, it turns out that emojis are built into Google Docs and can be used for a wide range of fun learning activities. In this chapter we will take a look at five sample ideas:

- Write a summary with emojis
- Create a rebus story with emojis
- Explore emotions with emojis
- Use emojis in place of math variables
- Create pictographs with emojis

NOTE

Emojis appear differently in different operating systems. For this reason, the images may not look the same on every device. If you are using any modern computer or device (Chromebook, Android, iOS, Mac OS, Windows), the emojis should display well. If you are using a version of Windows earlier than Windows 8.1, however, the emojis do not appear in color and many may be missing.

INSERTING EMOJIS

So how do you add an emoji to Google Docs? Since emojis are considered "special characters" in Docs, they can be added using the standard option for inserting special characters. Here's how:

1. Open a Google Doc as usual.
2. Click **Insert** in the top menu bar.
3. Choose **Special characters** . . . from the drop-down menu.
4. The **Insert special characters** window will open.
5. From the **Symbol** menu on the top left, choose **Emoji**.
6. You will see a grid of emoji images.
7. You can choose more emojis by choosing a **category** in the second drop-down menu. The categories include:
   - People and emotions
   - Animals, plants, and food
   - Objects
   - Sports, celebrations, and activities
   - Transport, maps, and signage
   - Weather, scenes, and zodiac signs
   - Enclosed

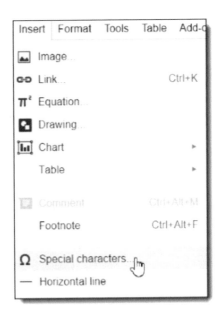

- Marks
- Symbols

8. If you **hover your mouse** over any of the emojis, you will get a pop-up window with a larger view of the emoji, along with its name.

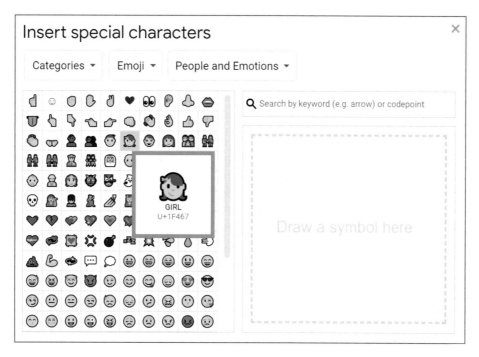

If you are not able to find the emoji you want easily, you can also **type in a keyword** in the search term box. If that does not work, you can even **draw a picture of the emoji** using your mouse in the box provided, and Docs will display suggested matches.

Whichever method you use, once you find the emoji you want, **simply click on it to insert it** into your Google Doc.

WORKING WITH EMOJIS IN GOOGLE DOCS

After you insert the emoji into your Google Doc, you can manipulate it in several ways. The thing to remember is that even though the emoji looks like an image, as far as Google Docs is concerned it is not really an image, but text. Emojis are just special characters.

For this reason, you cannot do to emojis the sorts of things you can do to images in Docs. That means you *cannot* do the following:

- Click and drag the corners to make the emoji bigger or smaller.
- Crop the emoji.
- Rotate the emoji.
- Turn on text wrapping so text goes around the emoji.

Since emojis are really just special text characters, you can manipulate them just like you would regular text.

But before I get into that, here's how to copy and paste the emoji:

1. Select the emoji and then copy as usual (select **Edit** then **Copy,** or right-click and **Copy,** or **Ctrl** and **C**).
2. Paste the emoji as usual (select **Edit,** then **Paste,** or **right-click** and **Paste,** or **Ctrl** and **V**).

And here's how to change the size of the emoji:

1. Select the emoji.
2. Change the size in the **Font size** drop-down menu in the top menu bar. You can also type directly into the font-size box to set your own custom size.

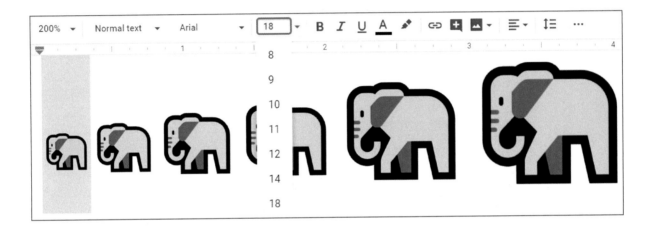

WRITE A SUMMARY WITH EMOJIS

Instead of having students write with words, let them express themselves with images. Students could use emojis to write a visual version of many traditional assignments. For example, students might:

*   Write the title of a book, story, movie, song, or play in emojis
*   Summarize what happens in a story with emojis
*   Explain a science concept or process with emojis
*   Retell a historical event with emojis

Using emojis in this way encourages students to determine the most important details or concepts, and then create a visual summary that clearly conveys those ideas.

As an example, here is my take on the title *Of Mice and Men:*

And here is my summary of *Charlotte's Web:*

And here is my emoji version of photosynthesis:

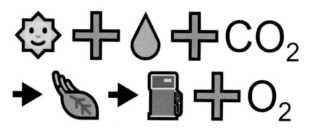

✏️ CREATE A REBUS STORY WITH EMOJIS

Instead of using all emojis, another option would be to write by combining text and emojis. This could be done to create a rebus. Anyone who grew up reading *Highlights* magazine in the dentist's waiting room will quickly recognize a rebus. Basically, it is a story where some of the words are replaced by images.

The 👧 went to the 🐖🏠 to get the 🥚🥚. The 👧 took the 🥚🥚 to her 👩. Then she got on the 🚌 to go to 🏫.

Although you can easily create rebus stories from scratch, if it is helpful you can also use one of several templates I have created, which can be found on the "Book Links" page of my blog.

Sometimes the images are further modified by adding or subtracting letters from them, as indicated in this example:

🐐-at 🐕-d 🍁-af

Again, this can be a fun activity for students, both to create and to read. It may even help with younger students who are not proficient at spelling but can choose the image for the word they want.

EXPLORE EMOTIONS WITH EMOJIS

As the name implies, emojis are especially good at expressing emotions. This can work well for activities in which students need to identify and explain feelings. For example, a student could identify the feelings of a character in the most recent chapter of the novel they are reading for class, or a movie they watched, or another story.

As an example, below is a Character Emojis Google Docs template that provides seventy-two emojis representing different emotions. Students can use the emojis to show which emotions a character feels in a book, story, movie, et cetera.

To do this, students click in a square with a chosen emoji, then click the **Background color paint roller icon** in the top toolbar to fill in the box with a selected color. When done choosing emojis, a student can then write an explanation of how those represent the character's emotions. The student can even color the text they write to match the colors they chose to fill in the emoji boxes. You can get your own copy of the Character Emojis Template on the "Book Links" page.

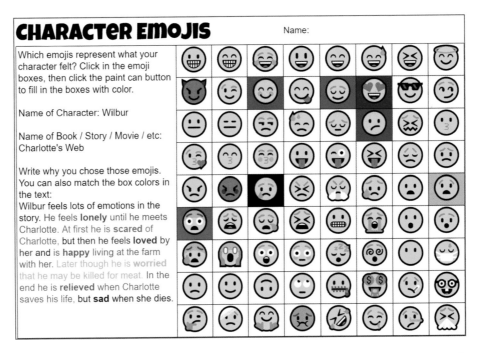

As needed, the template could easily be edited to accommodate other activities. For example, a student could work on self-reflection by expressing how they are feeling about the most recent lesson, class activity, assessment, or project by choosing appropriate emojis.

 # USE EMOJIS IN PLACE OF MATH VARIABLES

When I was a math teacher, I tried to make algebra more accessible for students in many ways. One concept I tackled was variables, as it was always a challenge for students to move from numbers to letters in math. Since a variable is just a placeholder for a number, though, variables don't just have to be letters. I would frequently use symbols, pictures, and other items for variables to help the students see them for what they were.

The same thing could be done with emojis. For example, here is the distributive property done with animal emojis:

$$3(2\, 🐔 +3\, 🐖)=6\, 🐔 +9\, 🐖$$

Basically, it says that if you have 3 barns that each have 2 chickens and 3 pigs, then altogether you have 6 chickens and 9 pigs.

CREATE PICTOGRAPHS WITH EMOJIS

Another mathematical use for emojis is creating pictographs. A pictograph is a bar chart in which the bars are made of images. For example, in a survey asking how many pets each student has, an emoji of a dog could represent one person answering the survey. You can see how this could look in a sample Google Doc accessible via the "Book Links" page.

To make a pictograph in Google Docs with emojis, do the following:

Number of Pets
How many pets do you have at home?

	🐕					
	🐕		🐕			
	🐕	🐕	🐕			
🐕	🐕	🐕	🐕	🐕		
🐕	🐕	🐕	🐕	🐕		🐕
0	**1**	**2**	**3**	**4**	**5**	**6**

- Create a Google Doc as usual.
- Add a title and a description of what the graph is showing.
- **Insert a table** with enough rows and columns to show all the data you have collected (you can always add or delete rows and columns if needed later).
- For the bottom row, type in the numbers or text to list what you are counting.
- In the rows above that, **insert an appropriate emoji** to begin building the chart.
- Once you have inserted one emoji, you can just **copy and paste** it as needed to finish building the chart.

RESOURCES

You can access the following digital resources for this project via the "Book Links" page of my blog:

- Wintertime Rebus Template
- Halloween Rebus Template
- Valentine's Rebus Template
- Character Emojis Template
- Pictograph sample document

7: Creating a Story with Branching Paths

Growing up in the 1980s meant reading loads of Choose Your Own Adventure books. They were fun, and a little scary, and you died pretty much every time, but they got lots of kids into books. Interactive stories with branching paths can be part of a great project to inspire student writing. They encourage the development of creativity, planning, cause and effect relationships, elements of a story, collaboration, and more.

There are many options for creating such stories digitally, including Google Slides, Google Forms, and Google Sites. Each method has its own benefits and challenges. In terms of ease of use, though, in my opinion using Google Docs is one of the quickest and easiest ways to create a Choose Your Own Adventure story. Benefits of using Docs for this purpose include:

- Most students are more familiar with Google Docs than any of the other tools.
- Docs makes it easy to add text, images, and formatting.
- Linking is easy using headings.
- The result looks and feels like a traditional book.

Sample Story

Many years ago, when I was a middle-school teacher, one project tasked students with creating an interactive story. One of those stories was *Dragon Quest*. A group of five students wrote all the text in this story and drew the pictures. I have simply taken the content and put it into an interactive Google Docs format.

Fair warning . . . as with all classic Choose Your Own Adventure books, most of the endings involve death, so this story may not be appropriate for the very young.

If you are brave, though, and ready to face the dragon, it's time for your adventure to begin. To access the example interactive Google Doc story, use the *Dragon Quest* link on the "Book Links" page.

Creating an interactive story with Google Docs is actually quite simple, using only four steps.

Planning

Regardless of which tool you use to write an interactive story, the more planning you can do at the beginning, the easier the process will be later. If your story becomes long, it can get increasingly complicated to properly link everything together. You can map out your story and all the branches using nontechnology, like sticky notes, or using technology tools, such as online diagramming or graphic organizer programs (such as Lucidchart or Google Drawings).

Whatever tool you use, be sure to end up with each page labeled with a unique title. The easiest option would be to just use page numbers for this purpose. These will come in very handy later when you want to link the pages in Google Docs.

WRITING IN GOOGLE DOCS

Once you are ready to begin writing, you can use many Google Docs features to create an exciting story:

1. Choose an interesting, but readable font for your text by clicking the **font menu,** then choosing **More fonts,** and then browsing to select a new font.
2. Add images by clicking **Insert,** then **Image ...,** or by dragging and dropping pictures into the Doc, or by copying and pasting images into the Doc.
3. Use **comments** to leave feedback and suggestions for your partners if you are writing the story as part of a team.
4. Click **Tools,** then **Voice typing...,** if you prefer to dictate your story and have Google Docs automatically type it for you.

PAGE BREAKS AND HEADINGS

Beyond the basics of Google Docs, there are some special steps you need to take in order to make an interactive story. One of these is the use of Page Breaks and Headings.

As people read through your story, they will get to the bottom of a page and be given two or more options to choose from. Depending on which option they click, they will jump to a different corresponding page. For this transition to function properly, you will need to use **Page Breaks and Headings**.

As you type up your story, when you get to the bottom of a page, where the branching choices are listed, you will want to insert a page break right after the choices. This will give you a clean break between that page and the next, where the story will continue. To insert a page break:

1. Click **Insert** in the top menu bar.
2. Then click **Break** from the drop-down menu.
3. Finally, click **Page break**.
4. Alternately, you can press **Ctrl** and **Enter**.

Next, at the top of each new page you will want to add a specially formatted heading. This is critical, because later we will need to add links between reader choices and destination pages. The only way to do this in Google Docs is by using Headings. Here's how:

1. First, type in some text at the top of the page. Probably the easiest option is to simply type in the page number, such as "Page 12." The key is to make the heading unique and understandable, since this is what you will link to later. The best option would be to use the same naming technique as you used when mapping out your story in the planning phase.
2. Next, select the text and click the **Style** button in the top menu. The button will probably be labeled **Normal text**.

3. From the drop-down menu, choose **Heading 1**.

4. This will now format the text with default Heading 1 formatting.

If you want your headings to look different from the default, you can customize them:

1. Make any changes you want to the text (font, font size, font style, etc.).

2. Then select the text again.

3. Click the **Style** button (which should be titled **Heading 1**).

4. Go to the **Heading 1** option in the drop-down menu, but click the **right arrow**.

5. From the pop-up menu, choose **Update Heading 1 to match**.

6. This formatting will be automatically applied to any other passages in the Doc that you've marked as "Heading 1."

 # LINKING PAGES

When you are done typing your story, inserting the page breaks, and making headings at the top of each page, you can go back through and link all the pages. This will make your story interactive, allowing the reader to click the choice they want at the bottom of a page, and then jump to the corresponding page to keep reading.

Here's how you add the links:

1. Scroll to the bottom of your page text, where you have the options for the reader to choose.

2. Select all of the text for one of the choices.

3. Now click **Insert** and **Link,** or click the **link** button in the top toolbar.

4. In the link pop-up menu, click on the **Headings** option.

5. This will show you a list of all the headings in your Google Doc.

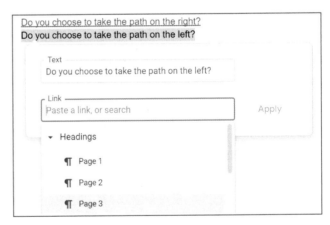

6. Scroll through the list of headings to find and select the correct page for that choice (again, this is why it is helpful to have your Headings named using an easily identifiable format, such as page numbers).

7. The text for that choice will be linked to the page you chose.

8. Repeat for the rest of the choices on that page, and the rest of the pages throughout your story.

Now your students' stories are ready to share.

RESOURCES

You can access the following digital resource for this project via the "Book Links" page of my blog:

- *Dragon Quest* interactive story example

8: REBOOTING YOU: POKE A STICK AT IT

What do you do when you don't know how to do something with technology?

A while back, I was leading a professional development session on Google Classroom for a roomful of educators. I had just finished explaining how you can invite a co-teacher to your class, and how they can make posts, create assignments, and grade work just like you. An attendee then asked me, "Can a co-teacher archive a class that is not theirs?"

Hmmmm . . .

As a Google Certified Trainer and Innovator, and a constant users of all of Google's apps, I try hard to know pretty much every nook and cranny of the Google tools. Of course, no one can know everything. I simply had never had an occasion to see if a co-teacher could archive someone else's class.

In short, I didn't know the answer.

What do you do when you don't know how to do something with technology?

This is something we all face from time to time. I face it as the "expert" standing in front of a room of teachers. You may face it as the teacher instructing a class full of students. Our students will face it all throughout their lives as they encounter new situations.

My solution is the response I gave to the teacher who asked the question, as well as to the entire room of attendees: *You poke a stick at it.*

Let me explain . . .

YOU CAN'T KNOW EVERYTHING

In life in general, and with technology specifically, you can't know everything. Technology (and Google Apps in particular) is a moving target, always introducing new tools and features. To use technology effectively, you have no choice but to be a lifelong learner.

So one of the first steps in dealing with a hole in your tech knowledge is to simply admit it. Some people think the three toughest words to say are *I love you* but in fact they are *I don't know*. Especially when we are in positions of authority, we feel we can't admit we may not know everything. We think we may look stupid or unqualified or unprepared. In fact, what we will look like is a learner.

Years ago, when I served as one of the leaders at a Google Teacher Academy, we were not called leaders. Instead, we were called Lead Learners. I love that mindset! We should always hope to learn something new, even when we are the ones leading professional development. I would go so far as to say that if you are not learning, you really are not engaging your audience, but are just on autopilot, giving a lecture.

If you want your audience (teachers, students, etc.) to learn, you need to model an attitude of learning, and you can't learn something unless you admit there are things you do not know.

We Learn Best by Discovery

So I admitted to my attendees that I did not know if a co-teacher could archive someone else's class. I was pretty sure they could not delete the class, but I really did not know if they could archive it.

So what could we do to find the answer? Certainly there were many options:

- We could Google it. Chances are a Google search would find one of Google's official help pages, or a useful blog post from someone's edtech site, or a forum question that a helpful person answered.
- We could post the question online to see if someone could help us. There are numerous Google-related communities, email distribution lists, and Twitter hashtags that would allow us to ask the question and crowdsource the answer.
- Or we could have shrugged our shoulders and given up.

Obviously, we didn't give up. My response to the attendees was, literally, "Well, I guess we need to poke a stick at it to find out."

Though there are many ways to get an answer, some options provide a much greater chance of learning, understanding, and remembering. I am a firm believer that self-discovery is the best instructor. Rather than just being told an answer, we learn so much more when we wrestle with the problem, test out solutions, and discover the answer for ourselves.

When I taught middle-school math, this was often the approach I took with my students. I could have just told them that when you add a positive and negative number you actually subtract the numbers and keep the sign of the larger one. Instead, we modeled the process of adding integers with colored chips, electrical charges, balloons, and bow ties (I will have to explain that last one sometime). The students then looked for patterns, saw connections, and discovered the rule. Whoever stated the rule first had the rule named after them, so for the rest of the year it became, for example, "Allison's rule for adding integers with different signs."

The point is that we learn best by asking questions, trying things out, solving problems, and discovering the answers ourselves.

The same is true with technology. If you don't know how to do something, just poke a stick at it. Try it out. See what happens. It is highly unlikely that you will actually break anything. And if you do, there is always the undo button or revision history or your friendly technology support staff.

So, if you want to see if a co-teacher can archive someone else's class in Google Classroom, try it out. Create a demo class, invite a colleague to be a co-teacher, and see if they can archive the class.

That's how I learn about technology. I don't have a degree in educational technology (my degree is in math), nor do I have any formal technology training. I just explore, click menus, see what happens, try things out, solve problems, ask questions, and learn. And you can, too!

WHAT ARE YOU TEACHING?

In the end, as a Google trainer I don't want to merely teach educators how to use Google tools. I want to teach them how to learn more on their own. I will be with them for only an hour or a day or a week at most (for those brave boot campers), but they have the chance to keep learning much more than I can teach them after I'm gone.

I encourage you to do the same:

- In your professional learning
- As an instructor of educators
- As a teacher of children

If you don't know something, embrace the opportunity to learn something new yourself, and to teach others the importance of learning through discovery.

So can a co-teacher archive someone else's Google Class? You'll just have to test it out yourself to see.

Go poke a stick at it.

SECTION 2

Rebooting Google Slides

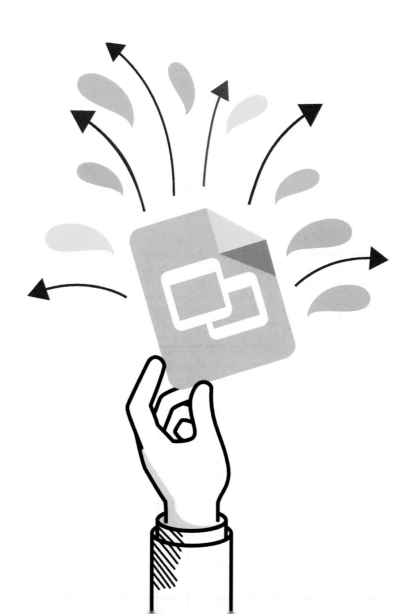

9: COLLABORDEPENDENT WRITING

Technology can have its pain points. Take peer feedback, for example:

- We want students to be able to write, express themselves, create, et cetera.
- Then we want students to be able to share what they made with their peers.
- Then we want those peers to be able to provide constructive feedback.

Normally we use Google Docs for a task like this. For the most part, it is an excellent option, but there can be some challenges. For example:

- If all twenty-five students in a class do their writing in their own Google Docs, we will need to find an easy way to share twenty-five different Docs, and we will need to open twenty-five different Docs to see everyone's work.
- Or, if all twenty-five students write in the same Google Doc, it can take some work to keep each student's writing separate and easily navigate from one student to the next.

What we need is an easy way for students to work independently when writing, but collaboratively when giving feedback. We need a tool that lets them work "collabordependently" (I assert this is a real word despite the red squiggly line that appears when I type it.)

Certainly Google Docs can do this, but sometimes it may be worth considering a different tool for peer feedback. That tool is . . . Google Slides. In this chapter I look at how Google Slides can be more than a presentation tool—it can become a versatile tool for collabordependence!

✎ PICK YOUR PROJECT

First things first, you will need to decide what you want your students to write, or explain, or create. Writing should be a key component of every subject area, at every grade level. Your project could be:

- A journal entry from a writing prompt
- A persuasive essay
- An argument for or against a position
- An explanation of a concept students are learning about in class
- A math story problem that covers content from the current math unit
- A story
- A poem
- A summary of a reading passage
- A retelling of an historical event
- And so forth . . .

CREATE A GOOGLE SLIDESHOW

Now that you have the topic in mind, go ahead and create a slideshow with Google Slides. You will probably want to include any necessary details about the activity at the start of the slideshow, including directions, a writing prompt, or resources to explore.

Directions:
- Create a new slide and then answer the question "Should cellphones be allowed in school?"
- Next visit three other slides and leave feedback with the "Comment" feature.
- Finally respond to comments left on your slide and revise your writing as needed.

STUDENT SLIDES

Next, you will want to consider your students' slides. The idea is for each student to have their own slide in the slide deck. Each student will use their specific slide to do their work, write, and so on.

If the students are older or more comfortable using Google Slides, they can simply create a new slide for themselves when they open up the app. To do this they would:

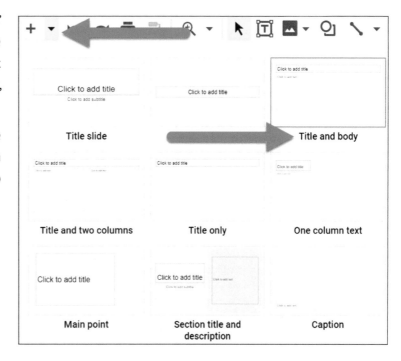

1. Click the **down arrow** next to the **plus button** in the top left corner of Google Slides.
2. Choose the type of slide they want to make. A good option for writing could be the **Title and body** slide.
3. The students can put their name in the title area and use the body section to write.

If the students are younger or less comfortable using Google Slides, you can create a slide for each student in the class ahead of time.

1. First, make one sample student slide.
2. You can use **Ctrl and D** to duplicate that slide as many times as you need for the entire class.
3. When students open the slideshow, they can pick a blank slide to work on. Or assign numbers to each student so everyone knows which slide is theirs.

If needed, you can go as far as adding in students' names on each slide ahead of time. If you're going to do this much work, you may want to consider making a master slideshow with all of the students' names on the slides and then simply make a copy of that slideshow anytime you want to do an activity like this.

In the end, how comfortable your students are with Google Slides will help you determine how much you want to set up ahead of time, and how much you want to let them do.

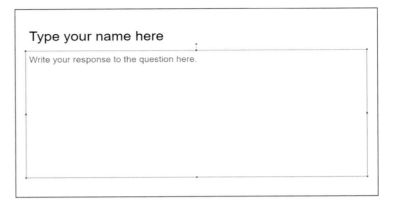

SHARING THE SLIDESHOW WITH YOUR STUDENTS

Now that the slideshow has been created, you need to share it with all of your students and give them edit rights to the slideshow. This will allow them to write on their particular slide. You can follow the usual steps for sharing, as outlined in the Introduction, but instead of making a copy for each student in Google Classroom you should select **Students can edit file** from the assignment creation screen. If you are sharing a link, select **Anyone with the link can edit**. Now when students open the assignment, they will all have access to the same slideshow and can edit their individual slides.

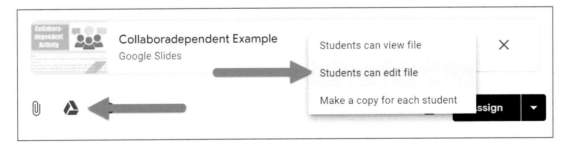

STUDENTS WORK INDEPENDENTLY

At this point, each student will go to their own slide in the slide deck and begin doing their work. This may involve writing a paragraph based on a prompt, or defining a scientific term in their own words, or explaining how to solve a math problem, et cetera.

During this process, the students can simply type, or they can take advantage of other features in Google Slides, such as inserting images, shapes, videos, and more.

Rick O'Shay

I think cell phones should be allowed in school because there are many educational things we can do with them. We can use the Google Classroom mobile app to take pictures and videos to submit. We can also use the Google Keep app to dictate notes and take pictures of things we need to remember. If a student uses their cell phone in a bad way, then maybe they should lose the privilege to have one, but those that do not should be allowed to use them in school.

✏ Students Give Feedback Collaboratively

When a students are done with their independent work on their slides, it is time for them to provide collaborative feedback for their peers. Students simply need to visit other slides in the slide deck to see what their classmates have written. To do this, each student would do the following:

1. Go to another student's slide and read what they have written.
2. Decide what feedback they would like to give.
3. Select the text or item on the slide they wish to comment on.
4. Click **Insert** in the top menu bar and then choose **Comment** from the drop-down menu.
5. Finally, the student can type their feedback in the comment box.

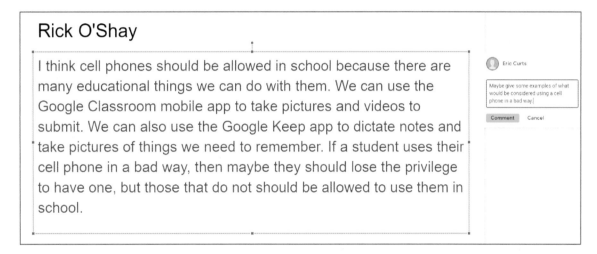

Students can check to see what feedback their classmates have provided them and make any necessary revisions to their work.

✏ Teacher Access

Because you created the slideshow, you have access to everything the students have written and the comments they have provided for their peers. Now you can easily click down through each slide in the slideshow to see all of your students' work in one convenient location.

One of the biggest challenges with a collaborative project is that students are able to edit each other's slides. This will likely happen at some point, either intentionally or by accident.

It is important that your students know that **version history** keeps track of every change ever made to a slideshow and who made the change. This feature will allow you to see if a student changes another student's work.

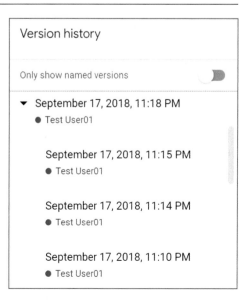

To access version history:

1. Click **File** in the top menu bar.
2. Choose **Version history,** then **See version history**.
3. You can expand and scroll through the history to see what changes were made by which students.

This is actually an important part of the learning process. In addition to learning how to create in Google Slides, it is important for students to learn how to work well together in a digital environment. This is a skill they will need all throughout their lives, in school, and in their careers.

10: DRAG-AND-DROP MANIPULATIVE ACTIVITIES

Another creative use for Google Slides is one that doesn't actually use it as a presentation tool at all, but instead as a work space for drag-and-drop manipulative activities and creativity. In such projects each student gets their own copy of the slideshow, then they can complete a learning activity in the slides by copying and pasting, dragging and dropping, inserting images, typing information, and more.

The best way to understand this is to start with the end in mind. Below are four examples of manipulative activities I have created with Google Slides. Each of these can be found on the "Book Links" page.

BUILD A SNOWMAN

In this activity students make their own snowman (or snowwoman) by copying and pasting eyes, mouths, arms, feet, and more onto a blank snowman. Then they write a story about their snowman.

BUILD A JACK-O'-LANTERN

As with the snowman template, in this activity students build a jack-o'-lantern and write about it. For an extension, students can also use the shape tools to draw their own custom mouths and eyes and such.

One Fish, Two Fish Sorting

This activity can fit nicely into Read Across America week to celebrate Dr. Seuss's birthday. Students can sort fish into Venn diagrams based on their color, size, and quantity. Students can also create their own sorting challenges.

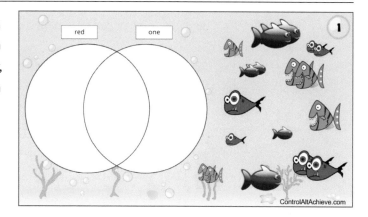

Long and Short Vowel Sounds

This final example goes one step further by adding audio clips to the slideshow. Students can play the audio to hear the word pronounced for each piece of clip art, and then drag and drop each image into the correct box for long or short vowels.

Building Your Own Manipulative Activity

The examples above can also serve as an inspiration to create your own drag-and-drop templates. Though many of my examples were geared toward younger students, these types of activities can be used with any grade level or subject area. For example, some projects for older grades could include:

- Arranging sentences in the correct order
- Placing icons on a map
- Putting the correct organelles in a plant or animal cell

Below are some tips that can be helpful for creating your own drag-and-drop activities in Google Slides.

Add the Background

Although you are making a drag-and-drop activity, there may be some portions of the slide you do not want the students to move. For example, when I made the "One Fish, Two Fish" template, I wanted the students to drag the fish, but not be able to move the Venn Diagram circles.

Unfortunately, Google Slides does not have an option for locking down items on the slide. Instead, the standard work-around is to make items a part of the background so that they can't be moved. Here's how I did that:

1. I created a new Google Drawing and set the page size to match the size of my slideshow (click **File,** then **Page setup**).
2. Next, I added all the content that I did not want to be movable in the final activity. This included an ocean background (from a free image site), the Venn diagram circles (from the **Insert** menu, choose **Shapes**), and some rectangle shapes where text would go later.
3. After creating the background, I saved it as an image by clicking **File,** then **Download,** then **PNG image**.
4. Back in Google Slides, I added this as the background by clicking **Slide,** then **Change background,** then uploading the image I had made.
5. Alternately, the background can be set by editing the Slide Master (click **Slide,** then **Edit master**).

✏ ADD THE MANIPULATIVES

After you have set the background for your slideshow, you can begin adding movable items. These could include clip art for the students to drag and drop into categories, or text boxes for them to rearrange, or shapes for them to copy and paste into something they are creating. Depending on the project, you can add manipulatives from many sources:

- Image search: Click **Insert,** then **Image,** then **Search the web** to find pictures to add.
- Explore tool: Click **Tools,** then **Explore,** then search for images.
- Free image sites: Many websites provide public domain or Creative Commons images that are free to use in your projects, such as pixabay.com. For an extensive list of free image sites, see the "Book Links" page.
- Shapes: You can add a wide variety of shapes by clicking **Insert,** then **Shape**.
- Text boxes: These can be added by clicking **Insert,** then **Text box**.

The items that you add can be placed in several locations, as needed:

- On the slide: You can add draggable items right onto the slide where the students will do their work.
- Off the slide: The gray area outside of the slide can also be used. Items can be placed in the area surrounding the slide, and then students can drag and drop them onto the slide for the activity.
- Another slide: If you have many items for students to work with, you may want to add them to a separate slide. The students can then copy and paste the items onto the activity slide.

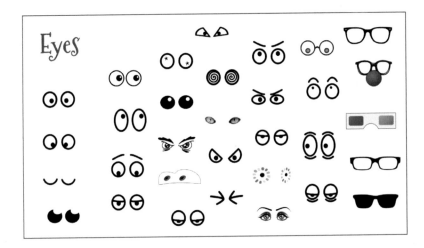

To add audio clips:

1. The audio files must be in your Google Drive—so if you saved them somewhere else, such as the Downloads folder on your computer, you will need to upload them to your Drive. For easy access, and to help with the next step, you should put all of the files in one folder in Drive.

2. Next, the audio files need to be shared so that anyone with a link can play them. This can be done file by file, but it is much easier to simply change the sharing permissions for the entire folder that holds the recordings.

With those steps completed, you can add audio from your Google Drive to Google Slides as follows:

1. With your Google slideshow open, click **Insert** in the top menu bar.
2. Choose **Audio** from the drop-down menu.
3. This will open up the **Insert audio** screen, where you can browse or search for the audio files saved in your Google Drive.
4. Choose the file you want, then click **Select** to insert it into your slide.

You can then share the activity with your students as outlined in the Introduction and they will be ready to go.

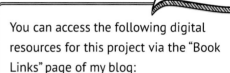

RESOURCES

You can access the following digital resources for this project via the "Book Links" page of my blog:

- Build a Snowman Activity
- Build a Jack-o'-Lantern Activity
- One Fish, Two Fish Sorting Activity
- Long and Short Vowel Sounds Activity
- List of free image sites

11: Video Mash-Ups

Mash-ups are a fun and popular way to express creativity, whether you are combining different styles of music, art, memes, or more. Mash-ups can also be educational when the creator uses two items to explain or express an idea, or uses one of the items to complement or expand on the other.

One fun way for students to try this out is by using Google Slides to "mash up" videos. Google Slides makes it easy to insert videos from either YouTube or Google Drive. Slides allows you to adjust your video options so that your videos automatically play when the slideshow runs. The end result is a presentation with two videos that play at the same time.

This could be used in several creative projects, such as:

- Adding music or popular songs to famous historical speeches, science videos, or scenes from a story
- Having one video explain a concept, while the other shows examples or demonstrations of that idea
- Showing contrast, by playing two videos that demonstrate different processes or ideas or time periods, for example

Below I explain how students can make mash-ups, and provide a free template they can copy and use, as well as a sample mash-up to show what a final product might look like.

THE MASH-UP TEMPLATE

Begin by getting a copy of the Google Slides Video Mash-Up template on the "Book Links" page. The template consists of the following slides:

- Title slide: Where the student can put in the titles of their mash-up videos
- Directions: Brief instructions for the student (this slide can be deleted after use)
- Videos: Where the student can insert the videos to be mashed up
- Explanation: Where the student can write about why they put these two videos together

INSERTING VIDEOS

Insert two videos on the Videos slide as follows:

1. Click **Insert** in the top menu bar.
2. Click **Video** from the drop-down menu.
3. From the **Insert video** pop-up window, you can search for a YouTube video, paste in the link to a YouTube video, or browse Google Drive for a video.
4. When you find the video you want, click **Select** to add the video to the slide.
5. As needed, move and resize the video.
6. **Repeat** for the second video.

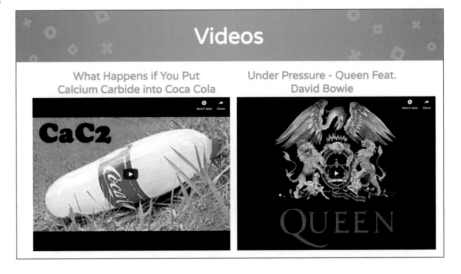

✎ Video Options

Now that the two videos are inserted, you will want to adjust a few options as follows:

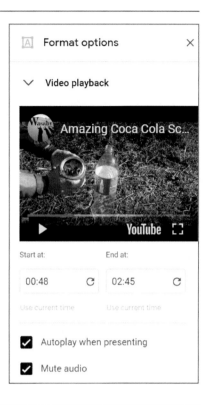

1. Click on a video to select it.
2. Click the **Video options** menu in the top menu bar.
3. The **Video options** side panel will open.
4. Check the box for **Autoplay when presenting** to force the video to play automatically when the slideshow runs.
5. Optionally, set the **Start at** time and/or **End at** time if you only want a portion of the video to play. This can be a good way to get the videos to sync up to only the segments you want to play together.
6. Optionally, check the **Mute audio** box if you want one of the videos to be silent.
7. **Repeat** for the second video.

✎ Add an Explanation

On the "Explanation" slide, students should write up why they chose the two videos to create a mash-up. This could include how the two videos relate to each other or how one video complements and expands on the other video or even how the two videos contrast with each other.

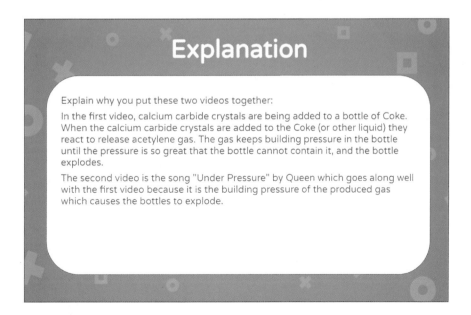

✎ PUBLISH TO THE WEB

When your slideshow is done, the easiest way to share it with others is to publish it to the Web. This will allow the slideshow to open full screen and start automatically. As usual, click **File,** then **Publish to the web**. Now click the **Publish** button and then **OK**.

Finally, **copy the link** provided for the published slideshow.

RESOURCES

You can access the following digital resources for this project via the "Book Links" page of my blog:

- Google Slides Video Mash-Up Template
- Video Mash-Up Example

12: Stop-Motion Animation

I have always been a giant fan of stop-motion animation. As a child I grew up watching *Rudolph the Red-Nosed Reindeer* and *The Year without a Santa Claus*. In more recent years I have enjoyed *The Nightmare Before Christmas, Fantastic Mr. Fox,* and *Kubo and the Two Strings.*

As much as I enjoy watching stop-motion movies, it can also be fun to create your own. With technology, there are many programs and apps to make the process much easier so that anyone can make a stop-motion animation.

One easy tool to use for this is *Google Slides*. We often think of Slides as just a program for creating multimedia presentations. However, with just a few tricks you and your students can actually use Google Slides to make stop-motion movies.

This can be a creative and fun way to:

- Tell a new story
- Retell a story read in class
- Reenact a historical event
- Demonstrate a scientific concept

- Explain how to solve a math problem
- Define a vocabulary term
- And much more

Stop-Motion Examples

For this activity, I created two examples of animation with Google Slides. One uses the more traditional approach of combining photographs, while the other uses shapes and text.

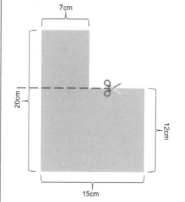

Example 1: Vocabulary Term: "Identical"

In my first example I used stop-motion to define a vocabulary term, in this case the word *identical*. To do this I used LEGOs to act out a scene (my own LEGO movie!). You can view the final product on the "Book Links" page.

Example 2: Area of an Irregular Shape

In my second example, I animated shapes and text in order to demonstrate how to calculate the area of an irregular shape. No traditional photographs were used for this example. To see this animation, go to the "Book Links" page.

One way to do this is to cut the irregular shape into several regular shapes.

✎ INSERTING IMAGES

If you want to go with the traditional approach for stop-motion animation, you will want to insert photos into your slideshow. Certainly these images can be taken with digital cameras or smartphones, but you can save a lot of time by simply using a webcam built into or connected to your laptop, Chromebook, or computer. Google Slides has a handy option that lets you insert images directly from your webcam.

1. Click **Insert** in the top menu bar.
2. Choose **Image** from the drop-down menu.
3. Choose **Camera**.
4. Click the camera button when ready, then click **Insert** to insert the photo into the current slide.
5. As needed, you can resize the photo to fill the slide.

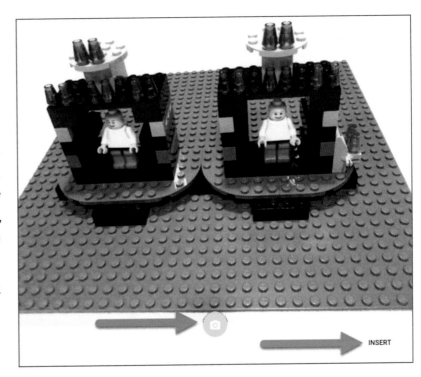

In between photos, you will want to make small changes to your scene. This could include moving your LEGO characters, clay models, action figures, et cetera. If needed, you can also move your webcam to zoom in, zoom out, or move around the scene.

Keep repeating this process to make all the slides you need to make your movie.

✎ INSERTING OTHER ITEMS

Instead of using photos, you can also create stop-motion movies by simply inserting and moving clip art, shapes, text boxes, and so on. Or you can combine these items with your photos by inserting them on top of your pictures.

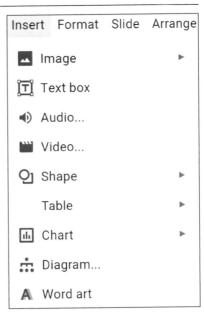

1. Insert items by clicking the **Insert** menu, then choosing **Shape, Text-box, Line, Word art,** or such.
2. When done, make a copy of the slide by clicking **Slide,** then **Duplicate slide**.
3. Now click on the items you inserted and make small changes to them to make it look like they have moved between slides.
4. This could include **moving an item, rotating items, or resizing** an item to make it bigger or smaller.

Keep repeating this process to make all the slides you need for your animation.

Below are some keyboard shortcuts to help make your changes between slides more precise.

Alt + left arrow	Rotate counterclockwise by 15°
Alt + right arrow	Rotate clockwise by 15°
Alt + shift + left arrow	Rotate counterclockwise by 1°
Alt + shift + right arrow	Rotate clockwise by 1°
Arrow keys	Nudge up, down, left, or right
Shift + arrow keys	Nudge one pixel at a time
Ctrl + alt + j	Resize smaller
Ctrl + alt + k	Resize larger

Making Slides "Last Longer"

When your slideshow runs, each slide will be shown for an identical period—it will "last" the same amount of time. Sometimes, however, you may want your movie to linger on a certain scene for a longer time. Although you can't make a specific slide actually last longer, you can make it look as if it does. The way to do this is to make multiple copies of the slide, without making any changes to it, so that it looks as if the scene is lasting longer:

1. Select the slide you want to last longer.
2. Make a copy of the slide by clicking **Slide** and **Duplicate slide,** or **copy** and **paste** the slide.
3. Repeat this multiple times to make five or ten copies of the slide (for example).

Later, when the slideshow runs, it will look like the movie has paused on this slide for longer.

Publish to the Web and Speed Up the Slideshow

By default, the "Publish to the web" link will open the slideshow full screen and start it playing, with each slide advancing every three seconds. That sounds quick, but it is way too long to give the illusion of animation. To make the stop-motion animation look like it is moving quickly, you need to edit the link to reduce the delay between each slide.

When you look at the "Publish to the web" link, you will see the following at the very end:

&delayms=3000

This tells the slideshow how many milliseconds to wait in between slides. There are one thousand milliseconds in one second, so the default of three thousand means there is a three-second delay before moving to the next slide.

You can speed up the slideshow by making this number smaller. For example, if you change the value to 250, that would be 250 milliseconds, or one-fourth of a second. This would mean there would be four slides displayed per second, which would be much faster and give the illusion of animation.

&delayms=250

You will need to experiment with different values to find the best speed for your slideshow to produced the desired effect.

Now that you have edited the "Publish to the web" link to make your slideshow move much faster, you are ready to share that link with others. Anyone who clicks the link will be able to view your stop-motion animation movie.

RESOURCES

You can access the following digital resources for this project via the "Book Links" page of my blog:

• My LEGO Movie Example
• My Irregular Shape Example

13: CREATING E-BOOKS AND COMIC STRIPS

Google Slides is an excellent tool for giving a presentation, but it can also be a creative way to tell a story. This can include making an e-book or a comic strip. Each slide of the slideshow could be a page of your book or a panel of your comic strip.

When you are done, the final product could certainly be printed out to make a physical copy, but it could also be shared and viewed online by anyone. If viewed online, the e-book or comic strip can also take advantage of features such as animation, transitions, and embedded audio for narration of sound effects.

Creating e-books and comic strips is a great way for students to:

• Retell a story they are reading in class
• Reenact a historical event
• Write an autobiographical account

• Visually explain a vocabulary term
• Illustrate a concept students are learning
• Provide commentary on an issue

A few examples of finished products can be viewed on the "Book Links" page of my blog.

✏ CHANGE THE PAGE SIZE

One of the first things to realize when telling a story with Google Slides is that the slide does not have to stay in the default landscape format. You are able to change the size of the slide to fit the product you are creating. For example, you may want a square slide for each panel of your comic strip. Or, as with a comic book I made called *Osmosis*, you may want an portrait layout for the book you are creating. You can change the dimension of your slides as follows:

1. Click **File,** then **Page setup**.
2. Now choose **Custom** in the **Page setup** window.
3. For the measurement units you can choose among **Inches, Centimeters, Points,** or **Pixels**.
4. You can now type in the **width** and **height** you want.
5. Click **Apply** when done and your slides will be resized.

Add Speech Bubbles

Pictures are a critical part of a comic strip or story, and images can easily be added to slides, as we've already learned. Speech bubbles, though, are a very specific image that is integral to these kinds of projects. They can be used in a comic strip or graphic novel to show characters talking to each other, as well as in e-books to provide helpful information. Google Slides has several speech bubbles, which can be inserted as follows:

1. Click **Insert,** then **Shape,** then **Callouts**.
2. Here you will find a variety of speech bubbles and thought bubbles.
3. Choose a shape and then click and drag to add it to your slide.
4. You can then double-click inside of the bubble to add your text.
5. Of course, the bubble and text can be formatted as usual with different colors, fonts, and more.

Add Transitions

For a fun effect, you can also add transitions between slides to make each new slide come in from the right to left, sort of like you are turning the page. Transitions can be added as follows:

1. Click **Slide,** then **Change transition.**
2. From the drop-down menu in the **Transitions** side panel, choose **Slide from right.**
3. You can adjust the speed of the transition with the slider.
4. Finally, click **Apply to all slides** to make this work for the entire comic strip or e-book.

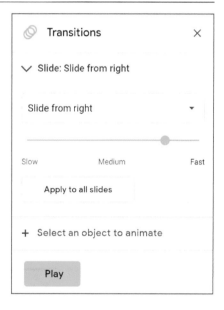

Add Audio

Another fun option for comic strips and e-books is to add audio to slides. This can allow the student to narrate their story or add sound effects to bring certain slides to life. An e-book I created, *My Pickup Has Hiccups,* uses audio clips to narrate the story. Below are the basic steps for adding sound to slides.

Get the Audio

First you need to either record the audio you want to add, or find and download the audio. There are a wide range of ways to record audio, but some free tools that work on Chromebooks include:

- Chrome MP3 recorder from HablaCloud
- Online voice recorder
- Beautiful Audio Editor
- TwistedWave

If you are looking for some good free sound effects, options include:

- SoundBible
- Zapsplat

For your convenience, links to these are available on the "Book Links" page of my blog.

Add and Share the Audio in Google Drive

Now that you have your audio, two things must be done with the files:

1. The audio files must be in your Google Drive, so if you saved them somewhere else, such as the Downloads folder on your computer, you will need to upload them to your Drive. For easy access, and to help with the next step, you should put all of the files in one folder in Drive.
2. Next, the audio files need to be shared so anyone with a link can play them. This can be done file by file, but it is much easier to simply change the sharing permissions for the entire folder that holds the recordings.

Insert the Audio in Slides

With those steps completed, you can add audio from your Google Drive to Google Slides as follows:

1. With your Google slideshow open, click **Insert** in the top menu bar.
2. Choose **Audio** from the drop-down menu.
3. This will open up the **Insert audio** screen, where you can browse for or search for the audio files saved in your Google Drive.
4. Choose the file you want and then click **Select** to insert it into your slide.

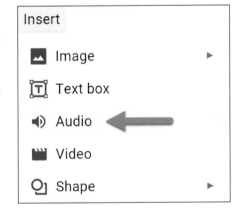

After the audio file has been added to your slide, you have several editing options for it:

1. Click on the audio file icon to select it.
2. Then, click the **Format options** button in the top toolbar.
3. Click **Audio playback** in the side panel that opens.
4. Here you can adjust settings such as:
    - Start playing **On click** or **Automatically**.
    - Set the **Volume level**.
5. **Loop audio** if you want it to keep playing after the slide has finished playing.
6. And select **Stop on slide change** if you want the audio to end when the user moves to the next slide.

RESOURCES

You can access the following digital resources for this project via the "Book Links" page of my blog:

- Sample comic strip: *Osmosis: Robot and Penguin Attempt to Explain This Science Concept*
- Sample E-Book: *My Pickup Has Hiccups*—with narration
- Sample E-Book: *Don't*
- Sample E-Book: *His Suit Was Hirsute*
- Links to free image sites
- Links to audio recorders
- Links to free sound effects

Ⓐ Format options   ✕

⌄   Audio playback

Start playing

◉ On click

◯ Automatically

Options

Volume when presenting

———————————————●

☐ Hide icon when presenting

☐ Loop audio

☑ Stop on slide change

14: INTERACTIVE SLIDES WITH PEAR DECK ADD-ON

It is no surprise that "death by PowerPoint" is a well-known expression. Whether it be PowerPoint, Google Slides, or any other multimedia presentation tool, we all know the potential boredom that can come from presenting with and learning from a slideshow.

Certainly we do our best to be engaging presenters, to include humor, interesting information, and maybe some animations to keep the audience's attention. Still, we know that our students will learn more if we can engage them and make the presentation more interactive.

Thankfully, we have just the tool for that: the Google Slides add-on from Pear Deck! This tool was already a popular resource on its own, but now with Pear Deck's add-on integration with Google Slides it is easier than ever to add true interactivity to your slideshows. Pear Deck is a great way to supercharge Google Slides, with many benefits:

- Every student can have a voice in answering questions and participating in class discussions.
- Students can see each slide on their device and follow along more easily.
- Students have a variety of ways they can express themselves, including open-ended text responses and freehand drawing.
- You can conduct quick formative assessments in class to check if students are understanding what is being taught.

WHAT IS PEAR DECK?

Pear Deck is a tool that integrates with existing slideshow apps to add interactive elements that allow the audience to participate, via the following:

- Multiple choice: Students are given a question with multiple answer choices, and they choose their response.
- Text entry: Students are able to type in text to response to a question.
- Numeric entry: Students can enter a number in response to a question.
- Drawing: Students are able to use drawing tools to sketch out their response.
- Draggable image: Students are given an image that can be dragged anywhere on the screen to respond to the question.

When the presentation runs, the slideshow displays on each student's device, with each slide advanced only when determined by the teacher.

The teacher is able to show the students' responses when desired. Responses can be shown individually or aggregated to look for patterns.

THE PEAR DECK ADD-ON

To install the Pear Deck add-on:

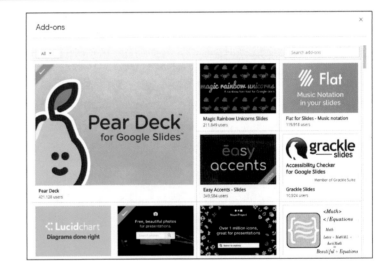

1. Open a Google slideshow as usual.
2. Click the **Add-ons** menu at the top.
3. Choose **Get add-ons** from the drop-down menu.
4. This will open the **Add-ons** window, where you can browse through the available add-ons.
5. When you find Pear Deck, click the **+FREE** button.
6. You will need to choose the Google account you are using, and then agree to the permissions by clicking **Allow**.
7. The Pear Deck add-on will be installed and will be available in your **Add-ons** menu from now on.

USING THE PEAR DECK ADD-ON

To use the Pear Deck add-on to make your slideshow interactive, you will want to start by building your presentation in Google Slides as usual, or by using a preexisting presentation. After you have the slideshow ready, you can go back through and add in interactive Pear Deck elements.

When adding interactive Pear Deck elements, you have two main choices:

- Add a premade interactive Pear Deck slide to your slideshow.
- Add Pear Deck functionality to an existing slide.

Begin by opening the **Pear Deck sidebar** (if it is not already open) by clicking **Add-ons**, then **Pear Deck**, then **Open Pear Deck Add-on**. The sidebar will open with options that include the following:

Template library: Here you will find premade interactive, templates. Simply click on a slide from the library and it will be added to your presentation. If needed, you can edit the slide after it is inserted to customize it for your class.

Ask students a question: Here you can add an interactive element to an existing slide, rather than inserting a new slide from the library.

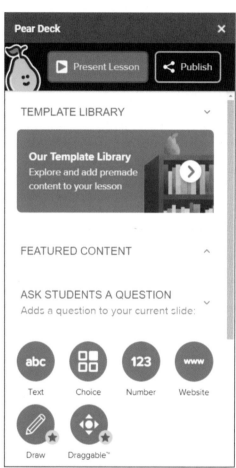

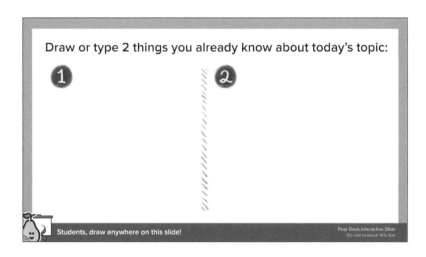

 # RUNNING THE PEAR DECK SLIDESHOW

Once you are finished adding interactive Pear Deck elements to your Google Slides presentation, you are now ready to run the slideshow, as follows:

1. Open the Pear Deck Add-on sidebar.
2. Click the **Present Lesson** button.
3. Your slideshow will be **imported into Pear Deck,** which can take a while if you have a lot of slides or large images.
4. You will get a screen with directions for your students to join your Pear Deck session.
5. Students will need to go to peardeck.com/join and type in the code displayed.

1. Once your students have joined, you can click the **Start Class** button to begin the session.

2. As you click through the presentation, your students' screens will show the current slide in sync with what you are displaying.

3. When you get to interactive slides, students will be able to type, draw, or drag as needed on their devices to respond to your questions.

4. You are able to show students' responses when desired by clicking the **Show Responses** button in the bottom right corner of the screen. Responses can be shown individually or aggregated to look for patterns.

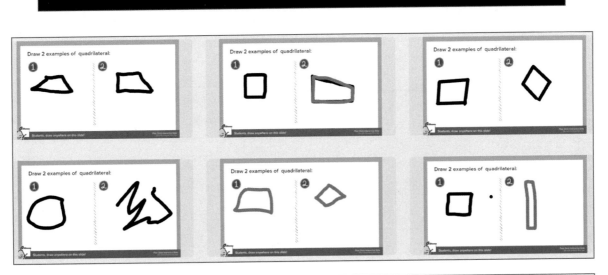

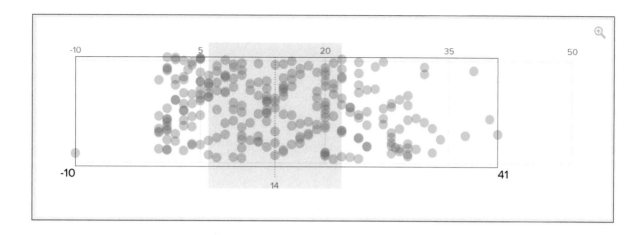

15: Nonlinear Slides for Stories, Quizzes, and More

Normally, a slideshow is designed to be viewed sequentially, one slide followed by the next, in order. However, Google Slides allows you to put **links** in slides that can link to any other slide in the presentation, regardless of order. By linking to other slides, a presentation can be nonlinear, allowing the user to choose which slides to view.

One possible use for this feature is to create a quiz for review purposes. One slide could ask a question and list possible answers. Each answer would be a link to another slide, where the user is told if they chose the correct answer or not. Helpful feedback could be included on the slides for the wrong answers.

Another possible use would be to create an interactive story, similar to an interactive story. One slide could tell a portion of the story, and then offer several story options at the bottom. These links would branch off to different slides to tell alternate storylines as chosen by the reader.

Another possibility would be to create a *Jeopardy!* game where the dollar amounts on the *Jeopardy!* board link to different slides with the questions, which then link to slides with the answers.

For examples of each of these, see the "Book Links" page.

When building a nonlinear slideshow, you should keep in mind a few special considerations. See below for details on how you and your students can create these activities.

JEOPARDY BOARD				FINAL JEOPARDY
Angles	Polygons	Graphing	Measurement	Funny Math
$100	$100	$100	$100	$100
$200	$200	$200	$200	$200
$300	$300	$300	$300	$300
$400	$400	$400	$400	$400
$500	$500	$500	$500	$500

NAMING SLIDES

When you create an interactive slideshow, you will need to create links to specific slides. This will be much easier if you name each slide in a consistent manner.

The name for a slide comes from the *Title* portion of a slide. When creating a slide, choose a slide layout such as *Title and Body, Title and Two Columns,* or *Title Only.*

Each of these layouts gives you a title box at the top of the slide. Whatever you type in the title section will be the name for that slide.

As an example, if you are making a quiz, the slides might be named as follows:

- Question 1
- Question 1: Answer A
- Question 1: Answer B
- Question 1: Answer C
- Question 2
- Question 2: Answer A
- And so on …

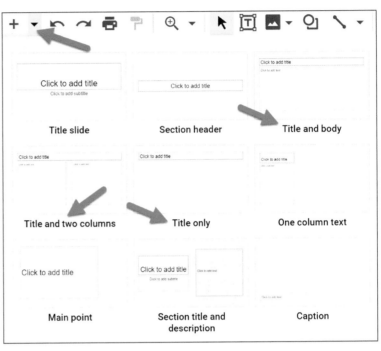

INSERTING LINKS

Before you can insert a link to another slide, you need to have the other slide(s) created to link to. So go ahead and make the source slide and the destination slide (or slides) that will branch off of it. Once you have the slides made, you can insert a link to a slide as follows:

1. Highlight the text, or select the object, that will be the link.
2. Click the **Insert link** button in the toolbar, or click **Insert,** then **Link**.
3. This will open a pop-up window.
4. In the **Link** box, click **Slides in this presentation**.
5. This will give you a drop-down list of all the slides.
6. Scroll through the list and choose the slide you wish to link to.
7. Click **Apply** when done.
8. The text or slide object will now be hyperlinked to the slide you have chosen.

If you need to change the link later, simply click on the linked text or object, and then click the **Edit link** icon to reopen the link window, where you can make any adjustments to the link as needed.

If you need to remove a link entirely, simply click on the linked text or object, and then click the **Remove link** icon.

✎ Avoiding Unintended Advancement

By default, if a user clicks anywhere on a slide, that tells Google Slides to move them to the next slide. Normally, you want this to happen, but not if you are making an interactive quiz or story. Instead, you only want the user to move to the slides you have linked, and to do so only by clicking the specific links you have inserted.

One option is to tell users to only click on the links, and hope that they follow your directions. There are some tricks you can use to help avoid this problem, though.

To avoid unintended advancement, you need to make sure everything else on the slide is actually linked back to the slide itself:

1. Click on an object on the slide, such as the title box, main text box, or an image.
2. Click the **Insert link** button in the toolbar, or click **Insert,** then **Link**.
3. This will open a pop-up window.
4. In the **Link** box, click on Slides in this presentation.
5. This will give you a drop-down list of all the slides.
6. Scroll through the slide names and **select the slide you are already on**.
7. Click **Apply**.
8. The slide object will now be hyperlinked back to the same slide itself, so if the user clicks on the item, they will stay on the slide instead of advancing.
9. Repeat for each item on the slide.

Besides clicking on items on the slide, users can also click on the background of the slide to advance. To avoid this you will need to insert a rectangular shape that covers the entire slide, link it to the same slide itself, and then move it to the back behind all the text and other objects:

1. Click **Insert** in the top menu bar, then choose **Shape**, then **Shapes,** then select the rectangle.
2. Click and drag a rectangular shape as big as the entire slide.
3. Make the shape link to the same slide you are on (as described above).
4. Feel free to change the color of the rectangle as desired, since it will serve as your new background. Simply click the **Fill Color** button (it looks like a paint roller) in the top toolbar to change the color.
5. Finally, move the rectangle behind all the text and objects by right clicking on the shape, choosing **Order,** and then **Send to Back**.

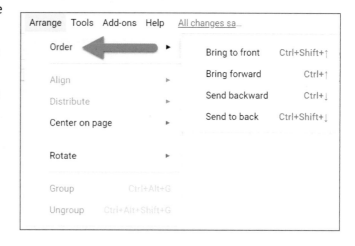

✎ DUPLICATING SLIDES

Because a lot of work needs to be done to each slide to insert all the links, it is not wise to create each slide from scratch. Rather, it would be most efficient to create a few complete slides, and then duplicate them as needed. You can then change the links that need to be adjusted, and edit the text for the slide, but will not have to repeat the entire process of inserting links for every slide you make.

To duplicate a slide, simply right-click on the slide thumbnail and then choose **Duplicate slide**.

✎ PUBLISH TO THE WEB

When the slideshow is complete, you will *not* want to share it using the Share button, because that would allow users to see all of the slides in advance. Instead, you want the slideshow to open in full-screen presentation mode. To enable this, you will want to use the **Publish to the Web** option discussed in previous chapters. In short, click **File**, then **Publish to the Web,** and then **Publish** to get the link for your playable nonlinear slideshow.

Reminder: Do *not* check the box for **Start slideshow as soon as the player loads,** since you do not want this slideshow to autoplay.

RESOURCES

You can access the following digital resources for this project via the "Book Links" page of my blog:

- Sample Interactive Quiz
- Interactive Quiz Template
- Sample Interactive Story: *Dragon Quest*
- Sample *Jeopardy!* Game
- 5-Topic *Jeopardy!* Game Template
- 6-Topic *Jeopardy!* Game Template

16: FLASH CARDS FOR RANDOMIZED QUIZZING

One of the first things every teacher wants to do each year is memorize their students' faces and names. This helps forge a personal connection to each of your students and helps them feel welcome and valued in your class. The last thing we want to do is call a student by the wrong name or resort to "Hey you."

When I was first teaching (back in 1992—you do the math), I took pictures of my new students on the first day of class using an old camera with 110 film. I would get the pictures developed at my local drugstore and then attach the photos to 4-by-6-inch cards on which the students wrote out their names and details about themselves.

These became my flash cards, so I could learn my students' names, faces, and key details about each of them. I would practice with these for the first week of school to make sure I learned about all 130 or so new students I had that year.

Now, with technology, there are so many better and faster ways to do this. As one example, I have created a Google Slideshow template that you can use to help learn your students' names and faces and something about them. You can even randomize the slides for better quizzing of yourself. See below to get your copy of the template and directions for how to use it.

You can also modify this template to create flash cards for a variety of activities, such as:

- Vocabulary words and definitions
- Key concepts and terms from your subject matter
- Learning a language with pictures and corresponding words
- Information about characters from a story or historical figures

Get the Template

On the "Book Links" page of my blog, you will find a link to the Google Slides template for Student Photos, Names, and More. When you click the link, it will make a copy of the template, and you will now have your own that you can use and edit as needed.

You will want to edit the first slide of the template to include your name and the name of the class. You can also delete the instructions slide if you want.

Since students will be editing the slideshow as a class, make as many copies as you need so each class period will have their own slideshow.

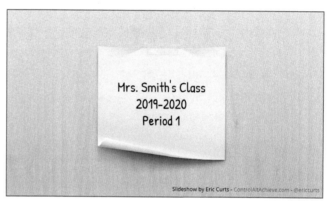

NOTE The template has animations added to the text and photo items on the student slides to help you learn their names when practicing. *Do not remove any of these animation settings.* This will be explained further below.

Share the Slideshow with Your Students

Next, you will want to share the slideshow with your students and give them edit rights. Your students need to be able to add a photo and enter text in the slideshow, so they will need edit access, at least at first. Follow the same instructions as outlined in the introduction, but if you use Google Classroom, choose **Students can edit file**. If you share a link, select **Anyone with the link can edit.**

Students Edit Their Slides

Each student will open the slideshow, choose a slide to work on, and enter their information.

1. Next to **Name**, they can enter their name.
2. Next to **About me,** they can write about themselves. Let the students know if there are specific details you would like here, such as interests, family, sports, pets, TV and movies, music, favorite subjects, et cetera.
3. Finally, students will add a photo of themselves to their slide.

The steps for inserting this photo are similar to the steps outlined in previous chapters, except that students will need to select **Replace image**. This method will replace the placeholder image with their photo (and will keep the animation order intact, which I will explain next). If students are using Chromebooks or a computer with a webcam, my recommendation for adding a photo is as follows:

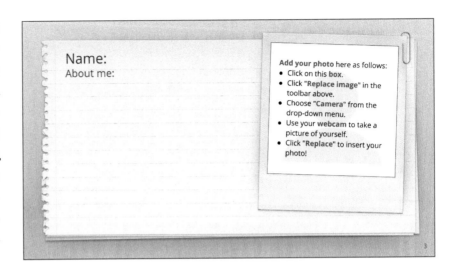

1. Have each student click on the **photo placeholder box** on the right side of the slide.
2. Next, click **Replace image** in the toolbar above.
3. Choose **Camera** from the drop-down menu.
4. Next, have students use their webcams to take pcitures of themselves.
5. Finally, click **Replace** to insert the photo.

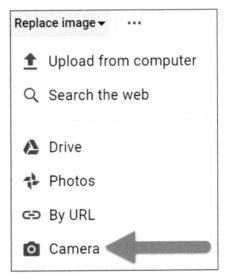

> **NOTE**
> If students do not have webcams they can always upload images as well. In that case, they should still follow the directions to **Replace image,** but should choose **Upload** instead of **Camera**.

As mentioned before, the template has animations added to the text and photo items on the student slides to help you learn their names when practicing. Make sure your students do not remove any of these animation settings.

✎ PRACTICE LEARNING STUDENTS

Now that you have the slideshow completed by your students, you can practice learning their faces, names, and more details.

1. First, begin by running the presentation as usual by clicking the **Present** button in the top right corner.
2. Click to advance the slides.
3. Each student slide has animations set for both the photo and text areas.
4. On the first click, the student's photo will appear. You can now test yourself to recall the student's name.
5. On the second click, the student's name and details will appear. You can now check yourself, and as needed you can remind yourself of the student's name and details.
6. Keep practicing until you have learned your students' names.

Randomize the Slideshow

For a bonus, you can also randomize the slides in your slideshow to help practice your students in a random order. One way to do this is to use the Slides Toolbox add-on to randomly shuffle the slides.

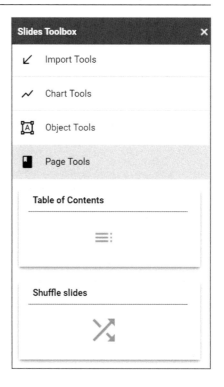

1. Install **Slides Toolbox** by clicking **Add-ons,** then **Get Add-ons,** and then searching for **Slides Toolbox.**
2. Click the **+ Free** button to install the add-on.

With the add-on installed:

1. Click **Add-ons,** then **Slides Toolbox,** then **Open.**
2. When the add-on panel opens on the right, choose the **Page Tools** section.
3. Next, click **Shuffle slides.**
4. Click **Yes** to randomly shuffle all the slides.

Now you can present the slides as usual to practice, but the slides will all be rearranged in a new order.

Animating Your Own Set of Flash Cards

The animation I have added to the template is integral to how these flash cards can be used, with the ability to shuffle slides. If you would like to make different flash cards (for learning vocabulary words, important historical dates, etc.) There are a few steps you will need to take to add animation to your content:

1. First, add all of the content to your slide, including text boxes, images, and such.
2. Next, click on the first item you wish to animate to select it.
3. Click **Insert** from the top menu bar, and choose **Animation**.
4. This will open a panel on the right side where you can choose which style of animation you want.
5. Select the option for **On click** so the user has to click the mouse to start each animation when they are ready.
6. Repeat this for other items on the slide you wish to animate.
7. If any of the animations are out of order, simply click and drag them in the panel on the right to put them in the correct sequence (such as question first, then answer).

You can access the following digital resource for this project via the "Book Links" page of my blog:

• Student Photos, Names, and More Slides Template

17: REBOOTING YOU: THE BIG BLANK WALL

I first began teaching in 1992 in Room 301 on the third floor of North Canton Middle School. It was an old building that had no airconditioning and few electrical outlets, but very high ceilings. In the back of my room was a row of lockers, and above the lockers was a good seven or eight feet of nothingness. Just a giant blank wall.

As a new teacher just out of college, I did not have much money to spend on room decorations. I needed something very big, and very cheap, to cover the large space. So I got creative. I spoke to the local movie theater and several local video rental stores (yes, we used to have lots of those). I asked if they could give me their old movie posters when they were done with them so I could use them in my classroom. They were happy to help out (perhaps it was pity), and soon I had a constant supply of posters.

The movie posters were a great way to cover the wall, brighten the room, and engage the interest of my students. Better yet, since I got new posters each month, I would give away the old posters as prizes that the students could earn. It was a great solution all around.

Several years later, something changed. To accommodate the growth in enrollment, our school district built a new high school. This meant our middle school would be moving to the old high school building, which for us was newer and bigger, and I would be moving to a new classroom.

My new classroom was very nice. It had airconditioning, brighter lights, more outlets, new whiteboards . . . and lower ceilings. As I unpacked and set up my room, I quickly noticed the problem. There was no big blank wall in my new room. How was I going to hang up my movie posters? I thought through the options. Maybe I could cover up one of the whiteboards, or perhaps I could hang the posters sideways—or could I possibly stick them to the ceiling?

And then it hit me. What on earth was I thinking? The only reason I had put up movie posters in my old classroom was to cover a giant empty wall, which I no longer had. Sure, the posters had served me well, had brightened the room, and provided the students with some rewards to earn. But they weren't my purpose—which was to create an engaging classroom. They were merely the means, or process, of achieving that purpose at the time.

I finally realized this about my movie posters. But I'll admit, it was difficult to let them go. I had come to rely on them as a way to decorate my room and motivate my students. They were safe and comfortable and part of my routine. But my world had changed, and it was time for me to change, and grow, and try new things.

It is a dangerous thing when we become so attached to a process that we lose sight of our purpose. This can land us in educational ruts or make us narrow-minded and resistant to change.

The same thing can be especially true with technology in education. For an example, consider printing.

Printing is a technological process that has gone through many changes over the course of my career. When I first began teaching we still had (I am not making this up) mimeograph machines. You know, the ones that you hand cranked, made everything purple, and emitted a headache-inducing smell. Since then I have seen printing evolve from personal DeskJet printers to high-capacity, high-speed network copiers that do double-sided printing, cover sheets, stapling, and hole punching.

And now the system is again being threatened by change. Over the last few years, we have been getting an influx of devices that don't communicate easily (or at all) with printing machines. We have Chromebooks, tablets, smartphones, and thousands of other bring-your-own-device items brought in by our students and staff.

And despite the benefits of these devices, some people are always quick to ask the famous question . . . How are they going to print?

But how about asking, *Do they need to print at all?*

If we go back to the ideas of process and purpose, we realize that printing is merely a process. The purpose it serves is to display and share student work, instructional content, and other information. And there are many, many processes that can do that now.

With Google Docs a student can write the rough draft of their term paper, digitally share it with their teacher, the teacher can add marginal comments for feedback, the student can edit the document, the teacher can see changes in the revision history, and the final product can be completed and graded without ever using a single piece of paper.

And information can be shared many ways other than printing, such as through presentations with Google Slides, videos on YouTube, posts on Blogger, web pages with Sites, live broadcasts with a Hangout, and much more.

We can run into what I'll call "big blank wall" thinking with many other processes.

Consider the purpose of providing instruction to students. The traditional process is to teach from the front of the class while students take notes. A new process may be flipping your class by recording your instruction on video through a screen-casting tool so that students can watch the lecture at home. Then you can help students work through the application of the material and dive deeper during class time.

Or consider the purpose of assessing student progress. Traditionally, our process has been based on paper-and-pencil tests, which take time to grade, and place an unfortunate time barrier between the test form and feedback. A new process for assessing progress can be to use Google Forms to provide students with online assessments, which can be graded automatically. By making quizzes digital, teachers can increase the frequency of formative assessments and students can get immediate, valuable feedback on their progress.

In all these situations, though, the purpose must remain the focus. No process in and of itself is either good or bad. It's only about tools. Because a process is old does not mean it is no longer valuable. Nor is every new technology appropriate for our needs.

The key, though, is to focus on the *why,* so we will be open to trying new *hows*. No matter how good our intentions, we are creatures of habit, and we can easily blind ourselves. When the big blank wall changes, we can't be so in love with our movie posters that we can't change as well. Because, whether we like it or not (or realize it or not), our educational world is changing. Changes in economic situations, changes in homelife, changes in future job opportunities, changes in current educational options: changes will always keep coming.

Though I missed my movie posters and big blank wall, the change pushed me to grow, and stretch, and discover new, exciting, and wonderful things. And of course, being a learner enabled me to become a better teacher.

So how about you? What big blank walls are changing in your schools, and what movie posters are you, or others, hanging on to? What new processes are available to meet the ultimate purpose of helping our students learn, grow, and be all they can be?

SECTION 3

Rebooting Google Drawings

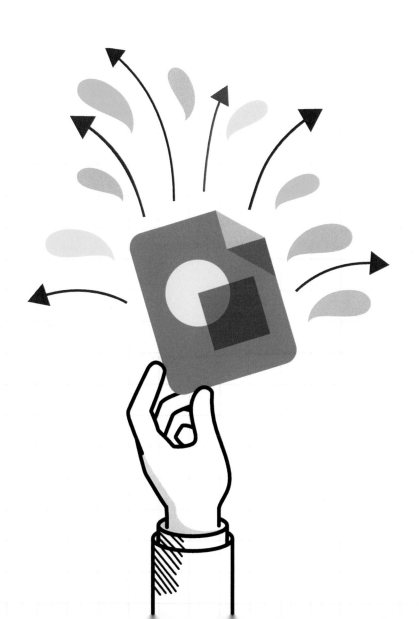

18: DESKTOP PUBLISHING

Although Google has loads of awesome tools, one thing that seems to be missing is a dedicated desktop publishing app to create brochures, newsletters, flyers, and greeting cards. (There are, of course, great third-party tools, such as Lucidpress.)

If you are willing to get a little creative, though, Google Drawings serves as a good option for some desktop publishing needs. Google Drawings is a very flexible program, allowing you to add text boxes, WordArt, images, shapes, and more to any part of a Drawing, and at any angle, much like a desktop publishing program would.

One such project you can do with Google Drawings is creating a poster.

✎ THE FINISHED PRODUCT: ELEMENTAL LOVE

Let's consider the end product to see what you can make with Google Drawings, and then go backward to take a look at some tips and tricks to help you achieve similar results. For this example, let's look at a poster I made out of a chemistry-themed poem that I wrote.

If you want to download a printable PDF version of the poster, feel free to use the links on the "Book Links" page of my blog. Below are some helpful options and ideas to use when creating a poster with Google Drawings. Again, Drawings is not a full-feature desktop publishing tool, but it is easy to use, and with a few tips and tricks, you and your students can make a creative final product.

Elemental Love

In the light of the Ag moon
With the stars and Hg above
I Pb you to a quiet place
And told you of my love

I drew a breath of O
And smiled brave and bold
With my Ne the ground below
I offered a ring of Au

With just a Ni to my name
You said "Yes" thereupon
I kissed you on your Cu lips
Now my lonely days Ar

Key
Ag = silver
Ar = argon
Au = gold
Cu = copper
Hg = mercury
Ne = neon
Ni = nickel
O = oxygen
Pb = lead

By: Eric Curts - www.ControlAltAchieve.com - @ericcurts

✏ CHANGE THE PAGE SIZE

One of the first things to realize is that you do not have to leave your Drawing canvas at the default size, which is 10 by 7.5 inches. Drawings allows you to adjust the dimensions to fit whatever project you are working on. For example, you may want your poster to be in portrait, rather than landscape orientation, or a larger size.

Here's how to change the canvas size:

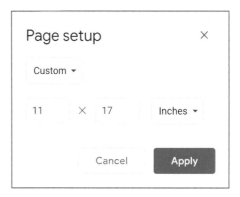

1. Click **File** in the top menu of Drawings.
2. Choose **Page setup** from the drop-down menu.
3. In the drop-down menu, switch from **Standard 4:3** to **Custom**.
4. For the measurement units, you can choose **Inches**, **Centimeters**, **Points**, or **Pixels**.
5. You can type in the **length** and **width** you want.
6. Click **OK** when you're done and your Drawing canvas will be resized.

✏ CHANGE BACKGROUND COLOR

Another change you may want to make for your poster is to select a different background color. By default, your Drawing starts off with a transparent background (it looks like a checkerboard pattern) so you don't have any color at first. You can change the background color as follows:

1. Right-click on a blank area of your Drawing canvas.
2. From the pop-up menu, choose **Background**.
3. You can now choose from one of the preselected colors.
4. Or you can click **Custom** to choose any color.
5. Or you can click **Gradient** to select a light-to-dark color blend.

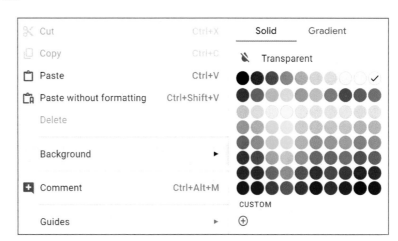

✏ INSERT TEXT

If your poster will have text, you can easily add that:

1. Click **Insert** in the top menu bar, then choose **Text** from the drop-down menu, or simply click the **Text box button** on the toolbar.
2. Now your cursor will change to a **plus sign** (+).
3. Go down to the Drawing canvas, then **click and drag** to create your text box (you can change its size and position later as needed).
4. Now type your text into the text box.

You can format the text using standard options, such as bold, italic, underline, font color, and font size. To really make your poster pop, though, consider changing the font face.

By default, you will only have a dozen or so font faces listed in your **Font** drop-down menu. But Google has provided over 900 additional fonts to choose from, offering most any look and feel you could possibly want. To access these additional fonts, do the following:

1. Click on your **Font** menu (it will probably display Arial as the default font).
2. Choose **More fonts** from the drop-down menu.
3. This will open the Web fonts window, where you can browse through hundreds of available fonts.

4. You can also narrow the list to show only **Display, Handwriting, Monospace, Serif,** or **Sans serif** fonts.
5. When you find a font you like, simply click on it to select it.
6. When you click **OK**, that font will be added to your font list and will be ready to use.

Below is a before-and-after example showing each of these changes to a text box.

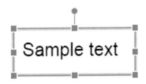

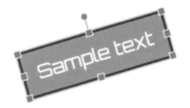

✎ INSERT AND EDIT IMAGES

Most posters will have graphics, and Google Drawings provides loads of ways to add images to your creation. As usual, you can add pictures by clicking **Insert**, then **Image**, or by clicking **Tools** and then **Explore**.

When you add images to your poster, you may need to edit them. There are several options for tweaking images.

- Move

Free move	Click and drag shape with mouse
Nudge	Arrow keys
Nudge 1 pixel	Shift + arrow keys

- Resize: To make the image smaller or larger, **click and drag** the blue squares in the corners of the image.
- Crop: **Double-click** on an image to go into crop mode, where you can **drag the black bars** on the edges to crop off portions.
- Crop to a shape: Select an image, then **click the down arrow** next to the **Crop** button in the toolbar to select a shape to crop the image to. This will cut out the image into the shape chosen.
- Rotate

Free rotate	Click and drag blue rotation circle
Rotate 90 degrees clockwise	Click **Arrange**, then **Rotate**, then **Rotate clockwise 90 degrees**.
Rotate 90 degrees counterclockwise	Click **Arrange**, then **Rotate**, then **Rotate counterclockwise 90 degrees**.
Rotate 15 degrees clockwise	Alt + left arrow
Rotate 15 degrees counter-clockwise	Alt + right arrow
Free Rotate by 15 degrees	Shift + click and drag blue rotation circle
Rotate 1 degree clockwise	Alt + shift + right arrow
Rotate 1 degree counter-clockwise	Alt + shift + left arrow

- Order: If you need to move an image in front of or behind another image, select the picture, then click **Arrange**, followed by **Move forward** or **Move backward**.
- Flip

Flip horizontally	Click **Arrange**, then **Rotate**, then **Flip horizontally**.
Flip vertically	Click **Arrange**, then **Rotate**, then **Flip vertically**.

✏️ ALIGN OBJECTS

If you have several elements on your poster, you may need to line them up consistently or divide them evenly across the Drawing. This can create a much more organized and professional look to the layout. This can be done as follows:

1. Select all of the items you wish to adjust.
2. Next, click the **Arrange** menu and choose one of the following:
   - **Align horizontally**: Line up all the items **Left**, **Right**, or **Center**.
   - **Align vertically**: Line up all the items **Top**, **Middle**, or **Bottom**.
   - **Center on page**.
   - **Distribute**: Space out the items evenly.

✎ EXPORTING THE FINAL PRODUCT

When you are done creating the poster, the final product can be shared in several ways:

- Share the Drawing using the **Share** button to make the poster available digitally to others.
- **Print** the poster directly from Drawings to hang up in your school.
- **Embed** the Drawing into a Google Site (from the **Insert** tab choose **From drive** to select the Drawing).
- **Export** the Drawing as a **PDF** (click **File**, then **Download as**) to give people an easy-to-use digital copy of the poster.

Download	▶	PDF Document (.pdf)
Email as attachment		JPEG image (.jpg)
Make available offline		PNG image (.png)
Version history	▶	Scalable Vector Graphics (.svg)

> **RESOURCES**
>
> You can access the following digital resource for this project via the "Book Links" page of my blog.
>
> - PDF of Elemental Love Poster

19: MOTIVATIONAL POSTERS

We are all familiar with motivational posters. They typically have a black background, one large image at the top, then a word or short phrase in large type below it, and finally a short inspirational sentence at the bottom. These motivational posters have been around for decades, and most likely can still be found in the classrooms, libraries, and offices of your schools.

Beyond just providing some encouragement to students, though, motivational posters can actually be part of a fun and educational activity. With some simple technology tools, students can create and share their own motivational posters. These creations can be used to show understanding of any concept being taught in your subject.

For this particular activity, Google Drawings is an excellent match. Drawings makes it easy to find and add an image, edit the text, change colors, and finally download or share creations. Students could create motivational-style posters for many educational activities. Some ideas include:

- Vocabulary terms
- Content area concepts
- Characters from a story
- People from history
- Events from history
- Foreign language terms
- Actual motivational posters

To make this even easier, I have created two templates (a horizontal poster and a vertical poster) that you and your students can use. Use the links on the "Book Links" page of my blog to get your own editable copies of these templates.

 ADD THE MAIN TEXT

After you have made a copy of the template, you can edit the poster. First, you will want to type in the main word the poster will address.

1. Simply double-click on the text box that contains the main word and edit the text as needed.
2. For stylistic purposes, you may want to put a space between each letter to stretch out the word a bit.
3. If needed, you can change the font size or font face as usual.

ADD SENTENCE TEXT

Below the main text of your poster is a spot for the sentence that goes along with the main text. Just like before, simply double-click on the text box and change your sentence about the main word to the sentence you want.

ADD AN IMAGE

Next, you will want to replace the template image with a picture of your choosing:

1. Click on the image and then click the **Replace image** button in the top toolbar.

2. You can select the new image as usual.
3. The image you choose will be automatically resized and cropped to fit into the space from the original image.
4. If you need to make any adjustments to the cropping or resizing, simply double-click on the image.
5. You can now click and drag in the center of the image to move it.
6. Or you can click and drag the corners to resize as needed.
7. Click off of the image when done.

ADJUST THE COLORS

Based on the image you have chosen, you may want to change the color scheme for the poster. Traditionally, for a motivational poster you would change the border color of the image and the text color of your main word.

- To change the border color of the image, click on the image, then use the **Line color** tool in the top menu bar.

- To change the text color of your main word, select the text, then use the **Text color** button in the top menu bar.

Sharing the Final Product

When you are done creating your motivational poster, you can share it using any of the methods described in this book's Introduction. In addition, since this is a drawing, you have the option to download your project as a JPG or PNG file.

RESOURCES

You can access the following digital resources for this project via the "Book Links" page of my blog:

- Horizontal Motivational Poster Template
- Vertical Motivational Poster Template

PETRI DISH

It's the only culture some people have.

20: Memes

Memes are everywhere. As a popular meme might say, "One does not simply go on the Internet without encountering memes." But if somehow you are not familiar with these ubiquitous images, a meme is a picture with superimposed text used to convey a message. Memes often have an element of humor, and the text usually follows a pattern based on the image chosen.

We see memes daily in social media posts, on websites, and in advertisements. They can also be used as a fun and creative tool for education. Memes can be used by teachers and students to:

- Define a vocabulary word
- Explain a science concept
- Give an opinion on a historic event
- Illustrate a theme from a novel
- Demonstrate a mathematical law
- Create class rules
- And more!

Rather than just using memes made by others, students can create their own to show their learning and communicate ideas. There are loads of tools that can be used for this purpose, but one great option is Google Drawings. This may be a good option for schools that block meme-creation sites, or that have concerns over the potential for inappropriate content to show up on a public site. Other benefits to using Drawings for this project are:

- Drawings works on PCs, Macs, and Chromebooks, though it would not work as easily on a mobile device.
- A small collection of images is provided.
- Drawings offers the option to upload or search for your own image.
- It is reasonably easy to use.

Fair warning, though—students will have a blast doing this project. So just brace yourself: memes are coming!

✏ USING THE MEME TEMPLATE

Certainly, students can use a blank Google Drawing to create their meme from scratch. If you want to save some time, though, or provide some assistance for younger students, using a meme template may be beneficial. Here's how it works:

1. First, get your own copy of the meme template on the "Book Links" page.
2. This will create and open a copy that you can edit.
3. To **change the text**, simply double-click on the text boxes and replace the sample text with your text.
4. To replace the image, simply click on the picture to select it, then click the **Replace image** button in the top toolbar.
5. You can add a new image in several ways, including **Upload from Computer**, **Search the web**, **Drive**, **Photos**, and **By URL**.
6. If you want to provide your students with some preselected images, I have included a link in the template to a Google Folder with a collection of common meme pictures. You can also access the folder through the link on the "Book Links" page.
7. When done, you can download the image by clicking **File**, then **Download as**.
8. Or you can share the Drawing with the **Share** button as usual.

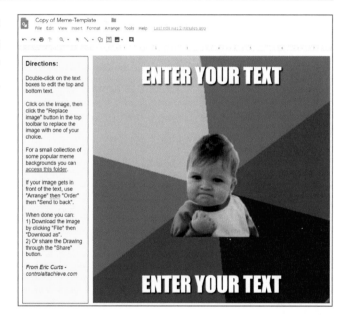

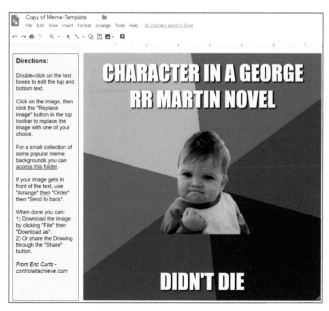

You can access the following digital resources for this project via the "Book Links" page of my blog:

- Meme Template
- Link to a Google folder containing preselected meme images

21: GREETING CARDS

Another fun desktop publishing task you can achieve with Google Drawings is creating greeting cards. This can be a useful project to help students work on their writing skills even as they develop their creativity. They could create greeting cards for real people (pen pals, reading buddies, parents, a partner class in a different culture or country, community members, and more) or they could create cards for fictional characters, people from history, or to celebrate important dates related to your subject area.

To help save time, I have created two Google Drawing templates that you and your students can use to get started. Use the links on the "Book Links" page to get your copies of templates for portrait or landscape greeting cards.

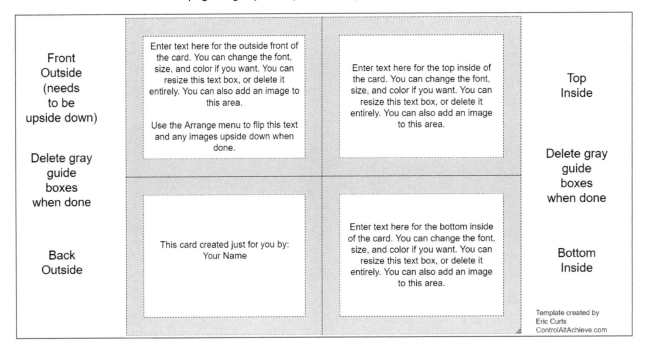

The template has been designed with four sections: the outside front, the outside back, the inside left, and the inside right (or inside top and bottom for the landscape version). For each section you can edit and format the text and insert images as needed to create your own greeting card.

 Editing Text

- You can simply double-click inside a text box to edit and add your own text.
- You can also select text and change the font, font size, text color, and other formatting.
- You can get additional fonts by clicking **More fonts** in the font selection menu.
- If needed, you can resize text boxes or remove them entirely.

Inserting Images

- You can add images to any of the four sections of the greeting-card template.
- You can click **Insert**, then **Image** to add an image as usual.
- You can move and resize images as needed.

Flipping Text and Images

Because the greeting card is going to be folded, two of the sections need to be upside-down for the portrait version, or one section needs to be flipped for the landscape version. For a portrait card, the inside left and inside right sections of the card need to have any text and images flipped vertically so that those sections will print upside down. For the landscape version, the front outside needs to be flipped. To flip text or an image:

1. Select the textbox or image.
2. Click **Arrange**, then click **Rotate**.
3. Choose **Flip vertically**.
4. Or choose **Rotate 90 degrees** twice.

Removing Guides

There are gray borders around each of the four sections of the template to leave room for margins and folding when the card is printed. When you are done creating the card, you will need to delete those gray borders.

1. Simply select each of the gray border boxes and press your **Delete** key to remove them.

✎ PRINTING

When you print your completed greeting card, make sure you let it fill the entire page:

1. Click **File**, then **Print**.
2. Choose your printer.
3. Be sure to check the box for **Fit to page** to make sure the greeting card covers the entire paper.

RESOURCES

You can access the following digital resources for this project via the "Book Links" page of my blog:

- Greeting Card Template (portrait orientation)
- Greeting Card Template (landscape orientation)

22: BACKGROUND-REMOVAL ACTIVITIES

A transparent image is a picture where some part of the image is see-through, as if that part of the image has been cut out. This is useful because transparent images look much better when combined with other images, allowing you to see the background or other items behind the picture. One fun activity you can do with transparent images is creating compilation pictures. This is where you take a background image to serve as a setting and then insert a new image on top of it to give the appearance that it is all one image.

For example, a student could put a picture of themselves into an event from history, a location in a foreign country, the setting of a book, or even a famous work of art. The student can also insert a speech bubble to share information about the scene.

BACKGROUND REMOVAL TOOL

In the past, if you wanted to remove the background from an image it was a largely manual process in which you would select and delete portions of the image bit by bit. Now, with machine learning, the heavy lifting can be done by computer.

One of the easiest tools for removing the background from an image is RemoveBG. It involves literally nothing more than uploading an image . . . and you are done! Here's how it works:

1. Go to the Remove BG website at remove.bg
2. Click **Select a Photo** to browse for the image you want to upload.
3. RemoveBG will process your photo and give you a new version that has everything removed except the person or people in the picture.
4. Finally, click **Download** to get your copy of the transparent image.

CREATING THE COMPILATION IMAGE IN DRAWINGS

Now that the student has an image of themselves without a background, they can insert themselves into a new image as follows:

You can access the following digital resource for this project via the "Book Links" page of my blog:

- Link to Remove BG website

1. Create a new Google Drawing.
2. Insert an image to serve as the background. Click **Insert**, then **Image**, then choose how you want to find your image.
3. Resize as needed to fill the background.
4. Next, insert the image with your cutout photo by clicking **Insert**, then **Image**, then **Upload from computer** (for example).
5. You can **resize** and **move** your cutout image as needed to position it in the Drawing.
6. You can also insert a **speech bubble** to share information about the scene. Simply click **Insert**, then **Shape**, then **Callouts** to choose a speech bubble you would like to insert.

For historical photos, you can adjust the colors of your image in Google Drawings to make it match better:

1. First, click on your transparent image to select it
2. Then click the **Format options** button in the top toolbar.
3. You can choose **Recolor** to change the color to one of the many preset colors.
4. Or you can adjust the **Brightness** and **Contrast** sliders as needed to make your image match the background better.

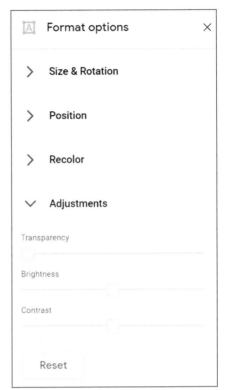

23: GRAPHIC ORGANIZERS

Graphic organizers are a great tool for sharing information, explaining a concept, or illustrating a relationship using elements such as images, shapes, text, colors, and connecting lines. Graphic organizers can be used in education with any age group or subject area. Some ideas for activities that use graphic organizers include:

- Creating a word study diagram
- Comparing and contrasting characters from a story
- Using a Frayer model to define a term in detail
- Exploring cause and effect
- Breaking down the parts of a story
- Organizing your ideas for writing
- Sorting words or images in a Venn Diagram based on characteristics
- Arranging items in their proper sequence

There are many excellent tools for creating graphic organizers. Some are programs that you install on your computer, while others are online. Some are free, whereas others carry a fee. Educators and students should be encouraged to try out many different tools to determine what works best for them and for specific situations.

One great choice for graphic organizers, though, is Google Drawings. See below for directions on how to create graphic organizers with Google Drawings. If you would prefer to use premade graphic organizers, you can access dozens of templates that I have made, which can be found on the "Book Links" page. In each template, there are directions off the left side of the Drawings canvas. Feel free to use and/or modify these as needed.

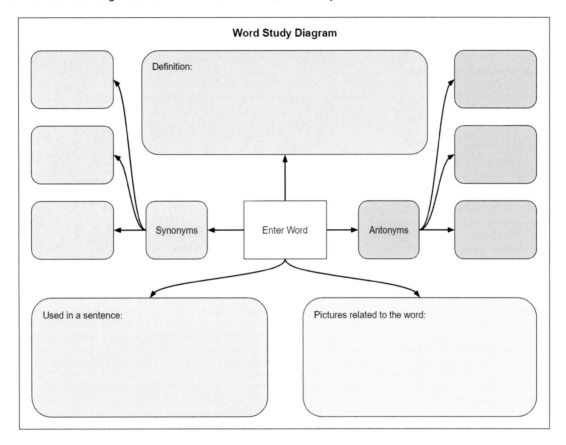

Word Study Diagram

Creating Your Own Graphic Organizer

Although there are loads of graphic organizer templates you can copy and use, it is also very simple for you and your students to create your own. This can give students the most freedom and will most clearly show their understanding of a topic since they will need to build their diagram and link the parts together themselves.

Below are some helpful directions for creating your own graphic organizer from a blank Google Drawing.

Page Setup

One of the first choices to make for the graphic organizer is the page setup. Depending on the graphic organizer to be created, a certain layout may be more or less appropriate. To adjust the orientation, dimensions, and background color, follow the same steps that you learned in Chapter 18.

✎ ADDING SHAPES

One of the most common elements of a graphic organizer is shapes. Boxes, circles, and other shapes can be used to hold text and can be connected to show relationships, cause and effect, details, and more. Google Drawings provides over 130 premade shapes that can be inserted into a drawing and then edited as needed. Using the shapes provided in Drawings (instead of inserting an image from a camera or the desktop) gives you more options to modify and change the shape. To insert a shape:

1. Click **Insert** in the top menu bar, then click **Shape** from the drop-down menu, or click the **Shape** button from the toolbar.

2. Next, choose the category— these include **Shapes**, **Arrows**, **Callouts**, and **Equations**.

3. Click on the specific shape you want.

4. Now your cursor will change to a **plus sign (+)**.

5. Go down to the drawing canvas, and then click and drag to create your chosen shape.
   Note: If you hold your **shift key** while dragging, the shape will keep its original proportions.

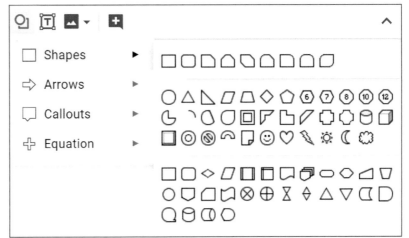

Once you have inserted your shape, you can modify it in many ways:

1. Click and drag the **square boxes** around the border of the shape to increase or decrease its size.
2. Click and drag the **circle** from the top of the shape to rotate it.
3. Click and drag the **yellow diamonds** (if available) to modify elements of the shape.
4. Click the **Fill color** button to fill the inside of the shape with any color.
5. Click the **Line color** button to change the color of the border around the shape.
6. Click the **Line weight** button to change the thickness of the shape's border.
7. Click the **Line dash** button to change the style of the shape's border.
8. Click the **Insert link** button to hyperlink the shape to a website or email address.
9. Most graphic organizers include text for categories, descriptions, details, and content. With Google Drawings you can insert text on its own, as outlined in Chapter 18.
10. Another option for adding text: insert text into the premade shapes by simply double-clicking inside the shape—a blinking cursor will appear in the shape and you can type in your text.

Below is a before-and-after example showing each of these changes to a shape.

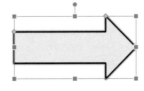
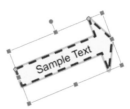

✎ ADDING CONNECTORS

The real power and purpose of a graphic organizer is to show how concepts are related to each other. This is most often accomplished by connecting the images, shapes, and text with lines or arrows to indicate relationships, cause and effect, sequencing, and more.

Google Drawings has two special tools for this purpose: the **Elbow connector** and the **Curved connector**. These differ from standard lines in Google Drawings in a few ways:

- They automatically snap onto the sides of your shapes, images, and text boxes.
- They automatically curve or bend to find the best path from one shape to another.
- When you move your shapes, images, and text boxes, the connectors stay attached to them.

To add a connector between two objects, do the following:

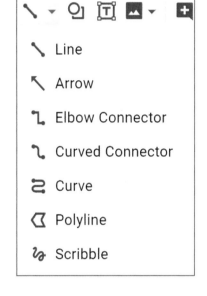

1. Click **Insert** from the top menu bar, then **Line** from the drop-down menu.
2. From the pop-up menu, choose either **Curved connector** or **Elbow connector**.
3. Your cursor will now turn into a **plus sign** (+).
4. Now hover your mouse over one of your objects and you will see that multiple **purple circles** will show around its edges. These are **connector points** for your line.
5. Click on the purple circle you want and hold down the mouse button.
6. With the mouse button held down, move your mouse over to the other object.
7. That object will now display **purple circles** for its connection points.
8. Hover your mouse over one of the purple circles and release the mouse button.
9. The connection will now be made between the two objects.

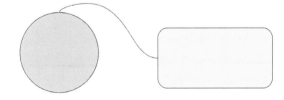

After you have attached the connector line, you can modify it in many ways. Simply click on the connector line to select it and then do the following:

1. Click the **Line color** button to change the color of the connector line.
2. Click the **Line weight** button to change the thickness of the connector line.
3. Click the **Line dash** button to change the style of the connector line.
4. Click the **Arrowhead start** button to change the beginning end of the connector line.
5. Click the **Arrowhead end** button to change the terminating end of the connector line.

Other possible modifications include:

- Switching between Curved and Elbow Connectors: click **Format**, then **Change connector**.
- Use shortest path for connector: click **Format**, then **Reroute connector**.
- Move connector points; simply click and drag the connector end to a different purple circle connection point.

24: Pattern-Block Activities

Pattern blocks are popular math manipulatives that seem to have been around forever (at least they were around when I started teaching math a couple decades ago). The standard set includes:

- Yellow hexagons
- Red trapezoids
- Blue thick rhombi
- Tan thin rhombi
- Green triangles
- Orange squares

Loads of fun learning activities can be done with pattern blocks, including exploration of symmetry, fractions, tessellations, angles, and more. Pattern blocks can also be used outside of math for creativity, art, writing, and so on.

As useful as pattern blocks are, the physical versions have a few drawbacks:

- They cost money.
- You will always have a limited amount.
- They can get lost.

One alternative is to use digital pattern blocks. Although there is nothing quite like handling the plastic blocks in real life, students can still do loads of activities with the virtual version.

To help with this, I have created a Google Drawings template with virtual pattern blocks. This is a Google Drawing with a blank canvas and one of each of the pattern blocks off to the left side of the canvas. Each of the six pattern block shapes and colors are accurately recreated in the template.

The pattern blocks can be copied, pasted, moved, rotated, and flipped any way you want for your learning activities (instructions can be found in the Desktop Chapter 18).

Sample Activity Templates

In addition to the blank template, I have also created several sample activities to show some ideas for how these could be used.

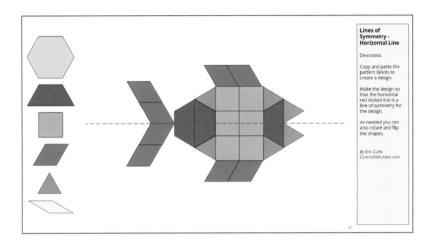

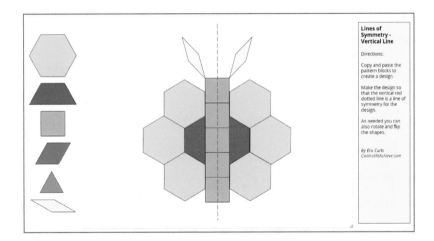

RESOURCES

You can access the following digital resources for this project via the "Book Links" page of my blog:

- Pattern Blocks Template
- Horizontal Line of Symmetry Activity
- Vertical Line of Symmetry Activity
- Ways to Make a Whole Activity
- Perimeter of a Garden Activity
- Biggest and Smallest Perimeter Activity
- Tessellations Activity
- Create and Write about a Picture Activity

25: MATH ACTIVITIES

Another great use for Google Drawings is teaching math. Drawings , with its shapes, rotations, tables, lines, and so on, lends itself very well to mathematics.

Below are some ideas for how Google Drawings could be used for students to explore and learn math concepts. For each activity you can find a template or example on the "Book Links" page. Feel free to use these templates as needed, or create your own math activities using some of the ideas presented here.

✎ LINES OF SYMMETRY

Students can create shapes or insert images, then add lines to show the lines of symmetry for those shapes.

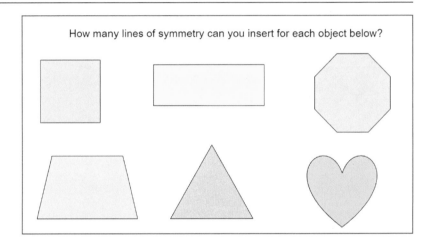

✎ SHAPES

Students can create a picture by inserting a variety of required shapes, and can then add colors and other images to complete their picture. Students could then use Docs to explain which shapes they used in the picture and where the shapes are.

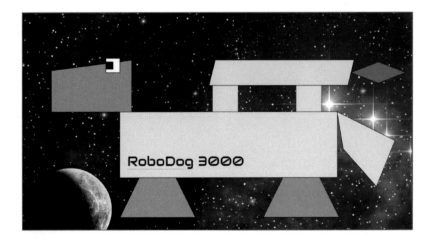

✎ Fractions

Students can create their own country flag using a variety of colored shapes—then they can use Docs to explain which fractional part of the whole each color represents.

✎ Pictographs and Line Plots

Students can insert a table, text, and images into a Drawing to create a pictograph or a line plot.

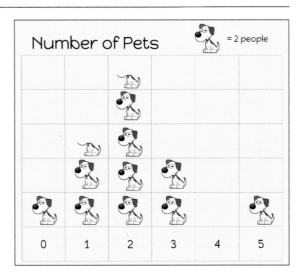

✎ Congruent Shapes

Students can use the tools in Drawings to move (translate), flip (reflect), and rotate shapes to determine congruency.

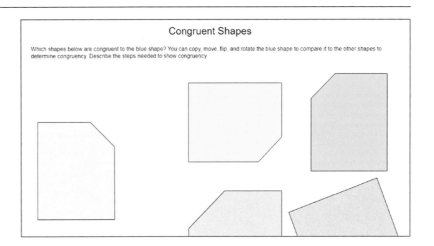

✎ ADDING INTEGERS

Students can represent an integer addition problem by using and combining colored chips that model the positive and negative numbers being added.

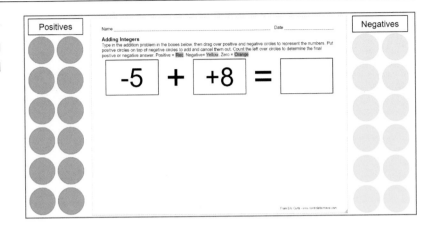

✎ ALGEBRAIC EXPRESSIONS

Students can copy and paste algebra tile shapes in the template to multiply algebraic expressions.

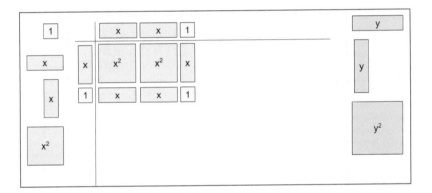

RESOURCES

You can access the following digital resources for this project via the "Book Links" page of my blog:

- Lines of Symmetry Template
- Shapes Template
- Fractions Template
- Pictographs and Line Plots Template
- Congruent Shapes Template
- Adding Integers Template
- Algebraic Expressions Template

26: STORY CUBES

Story cubes have long been a popular way to provide inspiration for writing. Although you can certainly buy these cubes, you can also make your own. Better yet, students can each make several story cubes and then you will have dozens and dozens to use for your class.

When making the story cubes, you have many options for what to put on the cubes:

- Some cubes may have characters on each face.
- Some cubes may have a location on each face.
- Some cubes may have an interesting object on each face.
- Or the cubes may have a mix of lots of different items or ideas.

When it is time to write a story, journal entry, poem, et cetera, a student can select several cubes (usually three to five). The student can then roll the cubes to see what items randomly come up on top of each cube. They can then use those images, emojis, or words to inspire their writing. Of course, these cubes can be used to create lots of other things besides story prompts. For example, you could make math cubes by putting numbers and operations on the faces.

One easy way to make your own story cubes is to use Google Drawings with pictures, emojis, or text. Below you can see the story cube templates that are also available on the "Book Links" page of my blog.

✎ STORY CUBE TEMPLATE—PICTURE VERSION

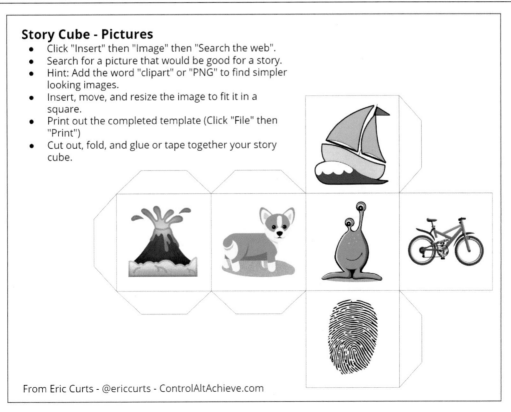

Story Cube - Pictures
- Click "Insert" then "Image" then "Search the web".
- Search for a picture that would be good for a story.
- Hint: Add the word "clipart" or "PNG" to find simpler looking images.
- Insert, move, and resize the image to fit it in a square.
- Print out the completed template (Click "File" then "Print")
- Cut out, fold, and glue or tape together your story cube.

From Eric Curts - @ericcurts - ControlAltAchieve.com

✏ STORY CUBE TEMPLATE—EMOJI VERSION

Story Cube - Emojis
- Double-click inside of each square.
- Click "Insert" then "Special characters" then choose the "Emoji" category.
- Find and insert an emoji that would be good for a story.
- Print out the completed template (Click "File" then "Print")
- Cut out, fold, and glue or tape together your story cube.

From Eric Curts - @ericcurts - ControlAltAchieve.com

✏ STORY CUBE TEMPLATE—TEXT VERSION

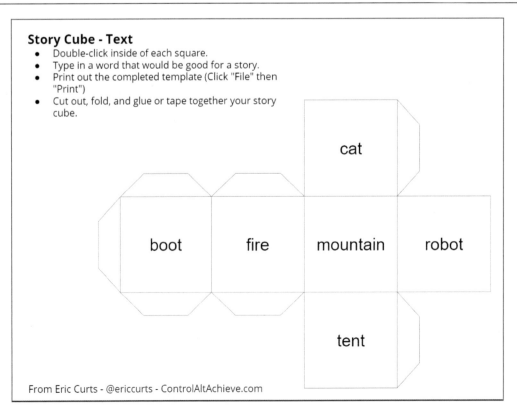

Story Cube - Text
- Double-click inside of each square.
- Type in a word that would be good for a story.
- Print out the completed template (Click "File" then "Print")
- Cut out, fold, and glue or tape together your story cube.

cat

boot   fire   mountain   robot

tent

From Eric Curts - @ericcurts - ControlAltAchieve.com

You can access the following digital resources for this project via the "Book Links" page of my blog:

- Story Cube Template—Picture Version
- Story Cube Template—Emoji Version
- Story Cube Template—Text Version

27: GOOGLINK INTERACTIVE IMAGES

Another educational use for Google Drawings is creating an interactive multimedia poster. This is very much like creating a Thinglink. Let's call it a *Googlink*. You can see many Thinglink examples at thinglink.com/featured.

Although Thinglink is an excellent tool, its free version does have some limitations. As an option, Google Drawings can be used very much like Thinglink, and it might be the perfect alternative for you and your students.

WHAT IS A GOOGLINK?

If you are familiar with Thinglink, you already know what a Googlink would be. Here is the gist:

- The user chooses an image they would like to annotate. This could be a diagram, a map, a painting, a photograph, et cetera.
- The user then adds icons on top of the image. These could be simple shapes, or they could be icons for videos, pictures, documents, Web links, et cetera.
- The user then adds a hyperlink to each icon, which links to a related resource that explains, elaborates, or further illustrates that portion of the image.
- The links might go to a video the student has recorded, a video on YouTube, a document the student wrote, a website, an online image, a map, a slideshow, or anything else that can be accessed online.
- The user then shares their final product so other people can click on the links to open related resources and learn what the user is explaining.

USES FOR A GOOGLINK

In school, students could create a Googlink as a fun and interactive option to show their learning of almost any content. Examples could include:

- The parts of an insect
- Key locations of a battle on a map
- Examples of geometric shapes in real life
- Their interpretation of different lines in a poem
- Steps in a lab experiment
- An "About Me" poster
- And much more!

Sample Googlink

As an example, I put together a very simple Googlink on the parts of a flower to demonstrate how this could look. Use the links on the "Book Links" page to test it out. Be sure to click on the various icons in the Googlink to open the linked resources.

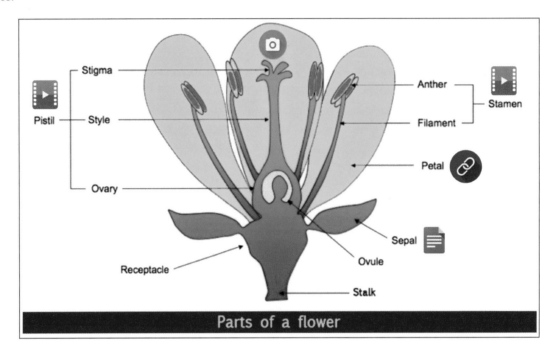

Creating a Googlink

Below are the basic steps for using Google Drawings to approximate a Thinglink.

Add the Base Image

After you have created a new Google Drawing, you will want to add the image you will be using for the base of your Googlink. This is the picture you will annotate with links to websites, videos, documents, other images, et cetera. If you need to resize your Drawing to match your base image, you can click and drag the bottom right corner of the Drawing, or you can click **File** and **Page setup**.

Add the Shapes and Icons

Next, you need to add the shapes or images on top of the background that people will click on to get to your related resources. You can add shapes or images using the standard methods.

✎ ADD THE HYPERLINKS

Now you want to add hyperlinks to the icons or shapes so they will link to your related resources:

- Click the icon or shape to select it.
- Next, click the **Insert link** button in the top menu bar, or click **Insert**, then **Link**.
- Paste in the link to the video, picture, Google Doc, website, et cetera.

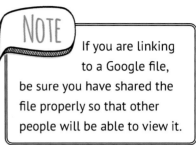

If you are linking to a Google file, be sure you have shared the file properly so that other people will be able to view it.

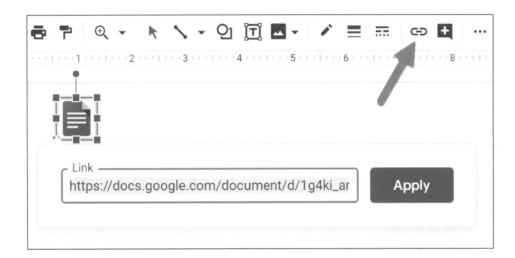

✎ SHARE YOUR GOOGLINK IN PREVIEW MODE

When you are done adding hyperlinks to your Drawing, you are ready to let other people view it. One option for this is to share the Drawing in a special Preview mode. Preview mode lets the Drawing open up full screen, rather than inside of the Drawings editor, but it does require a little trick:

1. Start as usual by sharing the Drawing as a link (Click **Share**, then **Get shareable link**).
2. Copy the shareable link and then make a small change to the end of the link's Web address.
3. Remove the end of the link that reads "edit."
4. Replace that with "preview."
5. Now when anyone uses that link, the Drawing will open up full screen and all your hotspots will be ready to be clicked!

```
https://docs.google.com/drawings/d/.../edit?usp=sharing

https://docs.google.com/drawings/d/.../preview
```

EMBED YOUR GOOGLINK

Another option for sharing is to embed your Googlink on a Google Site. When you add a Google Drawing to a Google Site, all the links in the Drawing stay live, so people can still click on them to open your related resources.

1. Open the Google Site webpage where you wish to insert the Googlink Drawing.
2. On the **Insert** tab, click **From Drive**.
3. Find and select the Drawing you created for your Googlink, then click **Insert**.
4. As needed, you can click and drag to resize the Drawing.

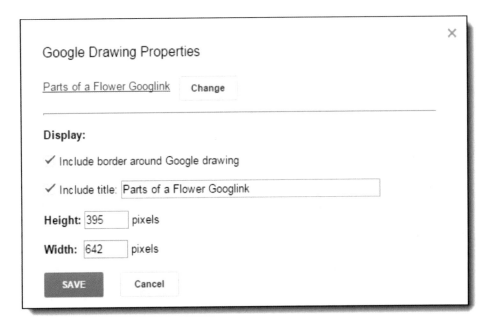

People will be able to view your Google Drawing on the site and click the links you have put inside of the Drawing. As always, though, make sure you have properly shared the Drawing and the Site as publicly viewable so people can access them.

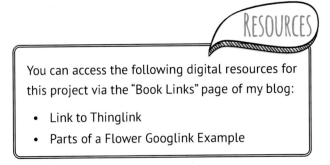

RESOURCES

You can access the following digital resources for this project via the "Book Links" page of my blog:

- Link to Thinglink
- Parts of a Flower Googlink Example

28: REBOOTING YOU: THE BIONIC EDUCATOR

As long as we have had technology and inventions and innovation, we have faced a question in education: Will technology ever replace a teacher? Or, to say it another way: Who, or what, is the best teacher in the world? A human? Or a computer?

For decades, people have asked if teachers would be replaced by videos, computer programs, the Internet, YouTube, or robots (like on the Jetsons).

We can laugh at these old visions of our future, but over the last twenty years we have seen science fiction start to become science fact. One of the biggest changes has come in the area of artificial intelligence (AI). Machine learning is fundamentally changing what computers are able to do. Just go back a couple decades to 1997 when for the first time ever a computer (IBM's Deep Blue) beat a chess Grandmaster (Garry Kasparov). This made some of us start to wonder if computers could truly replace humans.

Twenty years later, in 2017, an exponentially greater feat was accomplished as Google's AlphaGo AI took on Lee Sedol, the greatest go player in the world. If you are not familiar with go, it is a strategy board game for two players in which you try to surround more territory than your opponent. The reason this was more challenging for a computer "player" is that the number of possible positions on a go board exceeds the number of atoms in the universe. Unlike with chess, it is not possible to simply program all potential moves into the AI.

Instead, Google's Deep Mind team simply taught AlphaGo the rules of go, and then let AlphaGo play itself millions of times. And it learned the game on its own. When playing Lee Sedol, AlphaGo made moves that no human had ever seen before, or had even considered making. The AI used creativity and intuition to construct new knowledge. And AlphaGo won a game that no one had believed a computer could ever win. And again we asked: Can a computer replace a human?

So what do we do when faced with the rise of artificial intelligence? Do we give up? Do we ignore it? Do we fight against the technology?

Remember Garry Kasparov? When he lost chess to Deep Blue he was asked, "Does this mean that a computer is now the greatest chess player in the world?"

His answer is our answer.

He replied that the greatest chess player in the world is not a human—but the greatest chess player in the world is not a computer, either.

The greatest chess player in the world is a human using a computer.

Kasparov went on to create a new competition called advanced chess (also known as cyborg chess or centaur chess), where a human plays with a computer partner against another human-and-computer team, increasing the level of play to heights never before seen. And Lee Sedol, who lost to AlphaGo, took the same position as Kasparov. AI has expanded his understanding of the game and helped make him become the best player he could be.

So back to our original question: Who is the best teacher in the world?

It is not a human.

But it is also not a computer.

The greatest teacher in the world is a human using technology to its full potential.

When I was a kid, I loved watching *The Six Million Dollar Man,* the TV show about the "bionic man," a cyborg with superhuman strength. It has the great credo, "We have the technology. We have the capability to build the world's first bionic man . . . Better than he was before. Better, stronger, faster." Now, more than ever, we have the technology. To be the best educator you can be, to help your students be the best learners they can be, you need to embrace and use technology to reach our potential.

To be the best teacher in the world, you need to become a bionic educator. We have the technology. Let's use it to transform learning!

SECTION 4

Rebooting Google Sheets

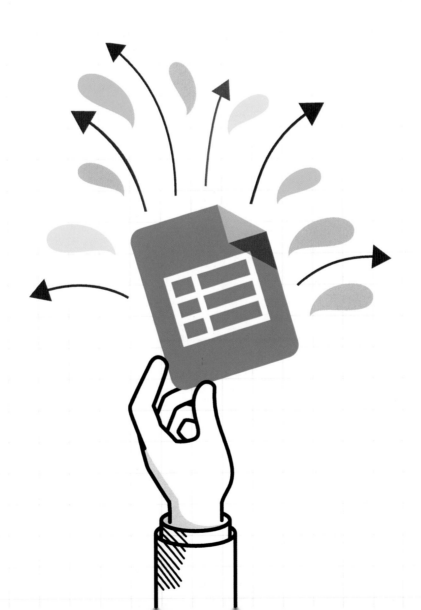

29: INTERACTIVE LEARNING DATABASES

Though we often think of Google Sheets as a tool for working with numbers, it can also allow students to create interactive learning databases.

Here's the idea. In your class, students have to process a large amount of data. Maybe this means:

- Characters in the novel they are reading
- Animals in their elementary science class
- Careers they are exploring in high school
- Countries they are studying
- Artists and the works they created
- Properties of geometric shapes

No matter what subject you teach, your students could benefit from creating a Google Sheets database. Using Google Sheets your students can:

- Collect important details as they are learning, such as key characteristics, facts, details, and information about the topics they are covering
- Build their own database of information, either individually or collaboratively.
- Organize, recall, and use the sorting and filtering features in Sheets to answer questions about the content, find connections, and better understand what they have been learning

See below for several examples from a variety of subject areas, as well as directions on how to build these spreadsheet learning databases and use the sorting and filtering tools.

EXAMPLE: CHARACTERS FROM A NOVEL

When students read a novel for school, there are a lot of characters to keep track of. This includes who they are, how they are related to each other, what they do, what changes they go through, and more. It can be a lot to make sense of.

One great way to manage all this information, make connections, and answer questions is by using a Google Sheet to collect character information. For this example I used the powerful novel *Wonder* by R. J. Palacio.

CHOOSE YOUR QUESTIONS

To begin this process, start by deciding what information should be collected. This could be something the class brainstorms and decides on, or could be details you choose ahead of time for the students. For the book *Wonder*, the items I chose were:

- Character name
- Character age/grade
- Character gender
- Is the character part of Auggie's family?
- Is the character nice to Auggie?
- Is the character mean to Auggie?

- Does the character change over the course of the novel?
- Does the character show up in Part 1 of the novel?
- Does the character show up in Part 2 of the novel?
- Does the character show up in Part 3 of the novel?
- Does the character show up in Part 4 of the novel?
- Does the character show up in Part 5 of the novel?
- Does the character show up in Part 6 of the novel?
- Does the character show up in Part 7 of the novel?
- Does the character show up in Part 8 of the novel?
- Your own notes about the character

Depending on the novel being read, these questions could be very different. Students might even want to add more questions as they read through the novel and come up with new ideas.

✎ Complete the Sheet

Once you have the questions, you can work on the Sheet:

1. Create a Google Spreadsheet as usual.
2. Add the questions in the first row, one question per column. You may want to abbreviate the questions to save space.
3. I would recommend "freezing" the first row so your headings will always stay at the top of the sheet when scrolling, sorting, or filtering later. To freeze the top row, click **View** in the top menu bar, then **Freeze**, then **1 row**.
4. As a student reads the novel, they will add characters to the spreadsheet, one character per row.
5. The student will fill in the columns with information about that character.
6. It may not be possible to fill in some columns right away, but these can be filled in as the student progresses through the story.
7. Each student can have their own Sheet to fill in, or this could be a collaborative activity where the entire class builds the spreadsheet database together.

You can visit the "Book Links" page of my blog to get your own copy of the Character Database spreadsheet I completed for the book *Wonder*.

	Name	Age	Gender	Family	Nice	Mean	Change	Part1	Part2	Part3	Part4	Part5	Part6	Part7	Part8	Notes
1	Name	Age	Gender	Family	Nice	Mean	Change	Part1	Part2	Part3	Part4	Part5	Part6	Part7	Part8	Notes
2	August Pullman	5th	Male	Yes			Yes	Yes	Yes	Yes	Yes	Yes	Yes	Yes	Yes	The main character.
3	Olivia Pullman	HS	Female	Yes	Yes	No	Yes	Yes	Yes	No	Yes	Yes	Yes	Yes	Yes	August's older sister.
4	Jack Will	5th	Male	No	Yes	Yes	Yes	Yes	No	Yes	Yes	Yes	Yes	No	Yes	August's best friend.
5	Summer Dawson	5th	Female	No	Yes	No	No	Yes	No	Yes	Yes	No	Yes	No	Yes	One of Auggie's first
6	Miranda Navas	HS	Female	No	Yes	No	Yes	No	Yes	No	No	Yes	Yes	Yes	No	Via's friend. Via, Mira
7	Justin	HS	Male	No	Yes	No	No	No	No	No	Yes	Yes	Yes	Yes	No	Via's boyfriend. He is
8	Julian Albans	5th	Male	No	No	Yes	No	Yes	No	Yes	Yes	No	Yes	No	Yes	The main antagonist
9	Isabel Pullman	Adult	Female	Yes	Yes	No	No	Yes	Yes	Yes	Yes	Yes	Yes	Yes	Yes	Auggie and Via's par
10	Nate Pullman	Adult	Male	Yes	Yes	No	No	Yes	Yes	Yes	Yes	Yes	Yes	Yes	Yes	Auggie and Via's par
11	Amos	5th	Male	No	Yes	Yes	Yes	No	No	No	No	No	No	No	Yes	5th grade student. A
12	Miles	5th	Male	No	Yes	Yes	Yes	No	No	No	No	No	No	No	Yes	5th grade student. A
13	Henry	5th	Male	No	Yes	Yes	Yes	No	No	No	No	No	No	No	Yes	5th grade student. A
14	Charlotte	5th	Female	No	Yes	Yes	No	Yes	No	No	Yes	No	No	No	Yes	5th grade student. Th
15	Mr. Tushman	Adult	Male	No	Yes	No	No	Yes	No	No	Yes	No	No	No	Yes	The director of Beec
16	Mr. Brown	Adult	Male	No	Yes	No	No	Yes	No	No	No	No	No	No	Yes	Auggie's first teache
17	Mrs. Albans	Adult	Female	No	No	Yes	No	No	No	Yes	No	No	No	No	No	Julian's mom. Does
18	Eddie Johnson	7th	Male	No	No	Yes	No	No	No	No	No	No	No	No	Yes	7th grade student wh
19	Mrs. Garcia	Adult	Female	No	Yes	No	No	Yes	No	No	No	No	No	No	No	Mr. Tushman's assis
20	Daisy	Dog	Female	Yes	Yes	No	Yes	Yes	Yes	No	Yes	Yes	Yes	No		Via and August's firs
21	Ximena Chin	5th	Female	No	No	Yes	No	Yes	No	No	No	No	No	No	Yes	5th grade student. D
22	Mrs. Will	Adult	Female	No	Yes	No	No	No	No	No	No	Yes	No	No	No	Jack's mom. She wa

✎ SORTING

Taking the time to complete the character spreadsheet will really help students to collect, organize, and remember important information from the novel.

But the real power comes now that the database has been built. At this point students can use the spreadsheet to make connections, draw conclusions, and answer questions.

Two tools that can help with this are sorting and filtering.

A common task when using a spreadsheet is to sort the records based on selected data. For example, in a spreadsheet you could sort by:

- Age: Group the different characters together based on their age
- Life expectancy: Sort animals in a life science spreadsheet
- Literacy rate: Sort countries in a social studies spreadsheet
- Salary: Sort jobs in a career search spreadsheet

To sort a spreadsheet, do the following:

1. Click in one cell inside the column you want to sort.
2. Next, click **Data** in the top toolbar.
3. Choose **Sort sheet by column A to Z** to sort alphabetically, or numerically, from low to high.
4. Choose **Sort sheet by column Z to A** to sort reverse-alphabetically, or numerically from high to low.
5. The rows in the sheet will now be rearranged based on the sort.

Data   Tools   Add-ons   Help
Sort sheet by **column A**, A → Z
Sort sheet by **column A**, Z → A

✎ FILTERING

Another tool to use with a set of data is **filtering**. This allows you to choose criteria to match, and then temporarily hides any rows that do not match those conditions. Filtering can be a powerful tool for taking a large set of information and reducing it to only the rows that match your interest. With this function, you could answer questions such as:

- Which characters go through a change over the course of the story?
- Are there any characters who are both nice and mean to Auggie?
- Are there any adults who are mean to Auggie?

Here is how you use filtering:

1. Click **Data** in the top toolbar.
2. Choose **Filter** from the drop-down menu.
3. A small arrow will appear in the top right corner of each column.
4. Click the **filter arrow** for the characteristic you want to filter by.
5. You will now get a drop-down menu, where you can check or uncheck the values you want to show.
6. Rows that do not match the values you select will be hidden.
7. You can repeat this process to filter by multiple columns to further reduce the rows shown.

For example, if you filter the **Age** column to only show **Adult**, and then filter the **Mean** column to show **Y**, you will get a list that shows only adults who were mean to Auggie. In this case, Mrs. Albans appears, which could spark some great discussion in class about how her attitude may have affected her son, Julian, who arguably is the person who is cruelest to Auggie in the entire story.

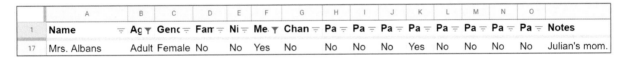

When you are done filtering, you can click **Data** and **Turn off filter**.

 OTHER EXAMPLES

You could also have students create interactive databases in Google Sheets for topics in any subject. Below are just a few examples. You can get copies of these examples on the "Book Links" page of my blog.

ANIMALS

In science class students could each research an animal and then fill in all the data for their animal in a shared class spreadsheet. Here is an sample spreadsheet:

Some possible questions to ask and investigate include:

- What animals live the longest?
- What is a mammal that lays eggs?
- What characteristics do all mammals have in common?

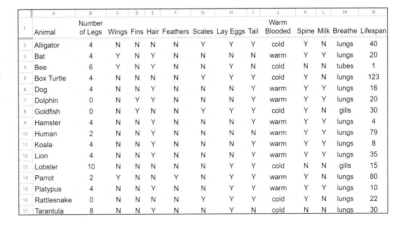

Animal	Number of Legs	Wings	Fins	Hair	Feathers	Scales	Lay Eggs	Tail	Warm Blooded	Spine	Milk	Breathe	Lifespan
Alligator	4	N	N	N	N	Y	Y	Y	cold	Y	N	lungs	40
Bat	4	Y	N	Y	N	N	N	N	warm	Y	Y	lungs	20
Bee	6	Y	N	Y	N	N	Y	N	cold	N	N	tubes	1
Box Turtle	4	N	N	N	N	Y	Y	Y	cold	Y	N	lungs	123
Dog	4	N	N	Y	N	N	N	Y	warm	Y	Y	lungs	16
Dolphin	0	N	Y	Y	N	N	N	Y	warm	Y	Y	lungs	20
Goldfish	0	N	Y	N	N	Y	Y	Y	cold	Y	N	gills	30
Hamster	4	N	N	Y	N	N	N	Y	warm	Y	Y	lungs	4
Human	2	N	N	Y	N	N	N	N	warm	Y	Y	lungs	79
Koala	4	N	N	Y	N	N	N	Y	warm	Y	Y	lungs	8
Lion	4	N	N	Y	N	N	N	Y	warm	Y	Y	lungs	35
Lobster	10	N	N	N	N	Y	Y	Y	cold	N	N	gills	15
Parrot	2	Y	N	N	Y	N	Y	Y	warm	Y	N	lungs	80
Platypus	4	N	N	Y	N	N	Y	Y	warm	Y	Y	lungs	10
Rattlesnake	0	N	N	N	N	Y	Y	Y	cold	Y	N	lungs	22
Tarantula	8	N	N	Y	N	N	Y	N	cold	N	N	lungs	30

CAREERS

Have students research careers they may be interested in. They could collect information on salary, expected job growth, educational requirements, and more. Here is a sample spreadsheet:

	A	B	C	D	E	F	G	H	I
1	Career	Salary	Hourly	# of Jobs	Outlook	HS	Bachelors	Masters	Education Requirements
2	Barber / Hairdresser	$23,200.00	$11.15	656400	10%	Yes	No	No	Graduate from a state-approved barber or cosmetology program and then pass a state exam for licensure
3	Commercial Pilot	$103,390.00		119200	5%	Yes	Yes	No	Commercial pilot's license from the Federal Aviation Administration
4	Dental Assistants	$35,390.00	$17.02	318800	18%	Yes	No	No	Graduate from an accredited program and pass an exam
5	Dental Hygienists	$71,520.00	$34.38	200500	19%	Yes	No	No	Associate's degree in dental hygiene. Programs typically take 3 years to complete.

Some questions to ask include:

- Which careers pay the most?
- Which careers will have the most job growth in the coming years?
- Of the careers that do not require a college degree, which ones pay the best?

FOUR-SIDED SHAPES

A student could record all the required characteristics for all the different types of four-sided shapes. This could include how many sides are parallel, if there are right angles, how many sides are equal, et cetera. Here is a sample spreadsheet:

RESOURCES

You can access the following digital resources for this project via the "Book Links" page of my blog:

- *Wonder* Character Database Example
- Animals Sheet Example
- Careers Sheet Example
- Four-Sided Shapes Sheet Example

	A	B	C	D	E	F	G
1	Shape	Number of Sides	All Right Angles	1 Pair Parallel Sides	2 Pair Parallel Sides	2 Pair of Equal Sides	All Sides Equal
2	quadrilateral	4	maybe	maybe	maybe	maybe	maybe
3	parallelogram	4	maybe	no	yes	yes	maybe
4	trapezoid	4	maybe	yes	maybe	maybe	maybe
5	isosceles trapezoid	4	no	yes	no	no	no
6	rectangle	4	yes	no	yes	yes	maybe
7	rhombus	4	maybe	no	yes	yes	yes
8	square	4	yes	no	yes	yes	yes
9	kite	4	maybe	no	maybe	yes	maybe

Some questions to ask include:

- Which shapes have the most restrictions?
- Which shapes have the fewest restrictions?
- Which shapes can't also be categorized as other shapes?

30: SELF-CHECKING ASSESSMENTS

Many excellent tools allow for online assessment, such as Google Forms, Quizlet, Kahoot!, Flippity, and Quizizz. In addition to providing teachers with data on student performance, online quizzes can be valuable simply for student self-assessment.

With self-assessments, the purpose is for the student to test themselves, see if they are correct or not, and usually retry until they get the right answer. Grades are not collected, because by the end the student should have every question correct. The point is to let the learner practice, see what they do and do not understand, and then work toward improvement.

One great option for self-assessment is to use Google Sheets with conditional formatting. This allows you to provide feedback based on what the student types in for their answers, so they can identify and work on questions they are struggling with. To help you get started, I have created a Self-Checking Assessment Template for Google Sheets.

 ## SELF-CHECKING EXAMPLES

Before we check out the template, it may be best to start with some completed examples to show the final product. For my examples, I used some Ohio trivia (since that is where I live). On the "Book Links" page of my blog you can get your own copy of either self-checking example (with or without hints).

Once you get your copy of the Ohio Trivia example, you can begin typing your answers in the Answers column. If you get an answer *correct,* the cell will fill in with green (because of conditional formatting, which I detail below).

	A	B
1	Questions	Answers
2	Capital of Ohio	Columbus
3	Nickname for the state of Ohio	
4	Year Ohio became a state	
5	Official state bird of Ohio	
6	The shape of Ohio's flag	
7	Ohio is an Iroquois Indian word meaning what?	

If you type in the *incorrect* answer, the cell will turn red. You can then try again until you get the correct answer.

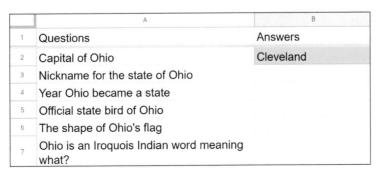

	A	B
1	Questions	Answers
2	Capital of Ohio	Cleveland
3	Nickname for the state of Ohio	
4	Year Ohio became a state	
5	Official state bird of Ohio	
6	The shape of Ohio's flag	
7	Ohio is an Iroquois Indian word meaning what?	

For the example that includes the Hints option, you can check the box to get a hint displayed, if needed.

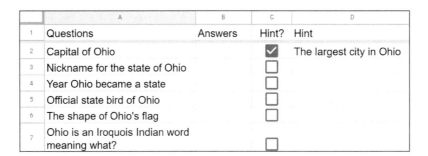

	A	B	C	D
1	Questions	Answers	Hint?	Hint
2	Capital of Ohio		☑	The largest city in Ohio
3	Nickname for the state of Ohio		☐	
4	Year Ohio became a state		☐	
5	Official state bird of Ohio		☐	
6	The shape of Ohio's flag		☐	
7	Ohio is an Iroquois Indian word meaning what?		☐	

SELF-CHECKING TEMPLATES

To make your own self-checking assessments, you can visit the Book Links page to get a copy of a template without hints and one with hints.

Once you have a copy of the template, here is how you fill it out and set it up for use:

1. The template will have two tabs at the bottom, one titled **Questions** and one titled **Key**.
2. Type in your questions on the **Questions** tab, one question per row.
3. Next, type in the answers on the **Key** tab, one per row, matching the rows on the **Questions** tab.
4. If you are using the template that includes the **Hints** option, type in the hints on the **Key** tab, one per row, matching the rows on the Questions tab. Hints can include text, links, images, and more.
5. When you are done, hide the **Key** tab by clicking on the arrow in the tab title below, then choosing **Hide sheet**.
6. If you need to un-hide the sheet later, you can always click **View**, then **Hidden sheets**.

When you are all done, you can share your Sheet with others with view-only privileges.

	A	B
1	Questions	Answers
2	Capital of Ohio	
3	Nickname for the state of Ohio	
4	Year Ohio became a state	
5	Official state bird of Ohio	
6	The shape of Ohio's flag	
7	Ohio is an Iroquois Indian word meaning what?	

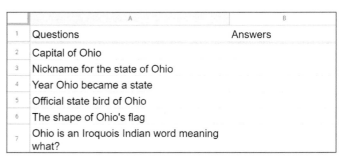

	A	B
1	Correct Answers	Hints
2	Columbus	The largest city in Ohio
3	Buckeye State	Related to the state tree
4	1803	In the 1800's
5	cardinal	
6	burgee	https://www.customflagcompany.com/blog/2015/3/4/shapes-and-styles-of-flags-and-banners

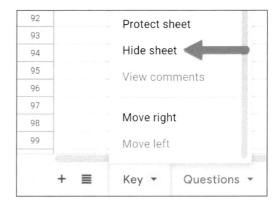

CONDITIONAL FORMATTING

For those interested in how the template actually works, note that the main feature of Sheets being used is conditional formatting. This is a setting in Sheets that allows you to *format cells based on the content that is typed into the cells.*

Here are the basics of how conditional formatting works:

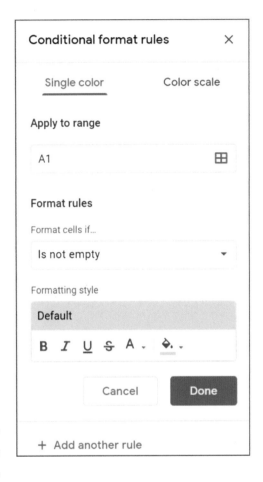

1. First, select the cell (or cells) you wish to apply the conditional formatting to.
2. Next, click **Format** in the top menu bar.
3. Choose **Conditional formatting** from the drop-down menu.
4. This will open a panel on the left titled **Conditional format rules**.
5. For **Apply to range**, you can change which cells are affected if needed.
6. For **Format cells if**, you can choose the condition that needs to be met. There are many options for this, such as comparing text, numerical values, and dates, as well as more advanced custom formulas.
7. For **Formatting style**, you can choose how to format the cells if the above-specified condition is met. This can include cell color, text color, bold, strike-through, and more.
8. If you need to add more rules, you can click **Add another rule** and repeat the process.
9. When you are all done, click **Done**.

Now anytime someone types content into the cells, the conditional formatting rules will be checked. If the content that is typed in matches one of the rules, the corresponding formatting will be applied to that cell.

For the Self-Checking Templates, I used custom formulas in conditional formatting to take what the user types in the Questions tab and compare that to the correct answers on the Key tab. If they match, the conditional formatting colors the cells in green, and if they do not match the rule colors the cell red.

You can access the following digital resources for this project via the "Book Links" page of my blog:

- Ohio Trivia (without hints)
- Ohio Trivia (with hints)
- Self-Checking Template (without hints)
- Self-Checking Template (with hints)

31: PIXEL ART ACTIVITIES

Growing up with video games in the 1970s and 1980s, I was well aware of pixels. When video games first started out, the screen resolution was so low that all your game characters and items were made of big, blocky squares called pixels. With some imagination, we could see a jumping plumber or a flying spaceship in those 8-by-8-inch or 16-by-16-inch grids of colored dots.

Today, video games are so hyperrealistic that you can't tell if you are watching a real-life video or a computer simulation. Everything old is new again, though, so there has been a resurgence of love for retro games and nostalgia for their antiquated pixelated style.

And so we have pixel art, which consists of making images from a small grid with a limited number of colors. And because you are filling in a grid with colors, Google Sheets is a great tool for making pixel art. Although this can be done by resizing cells to make the squares, and using the **Paint roller tool** to add colors, you can save a lot of time by using conditional formatting. To help with this, I have created a Twenty-Color Pixel Art Template, which includes several built-in activities. We will also look at directions for how to use and modify the template as needed for a variety of activities.

CONDITIONAL FORMATTING

There are many ways you can set up a Google Sheet for creating pixel art. You could use the **Fill color tool** to choose a color for a cell, or you could use the **Paint format button** or the copy and paste option to copy a color to other cells.

For this template, though, Conditional formatting is used to make the process as easy as possible for the end user. Conditional formatting, as covered in Chapter 29, is when you set up rules for the Sheet to format cells based upon what you type into them. For this template, I have created conditional formatting rules that will fill in the cells with specific colors based on the lower-case letter you type in, from *a* to *s*.

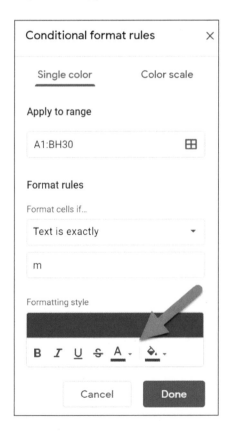

Though I have provided a diverse range of twenty common colors to use, you may find that you want or need to change some of the colors for the particular art you are working on. You can change the conditional formatting rules to change the colors as needed:

1. Click **Format** in the top menu bar.
2. Choose **Conditional formatting** from the drop-down menu.
3. This will open the **Conditional formatting panel** on the right side of the screen.
4. Scroll down through the rules to find the color you want to change.
5. Click on that rule to go into edit mode.
6. Click the **Text color** button and the Fill color button to choose the new color you want to correspond to the letter for that rule.

7. Click **Done** when you are finished.
8. Any cells with that letter will now be updated with the new color you chose.

20-Color Pixel Art Template

To get a copy of the Twenty-Color Pixel Art Template, use the link on the "Book Link" page of my blog. The template is made of several Google Sheets tabs. Here are the different tabs you will find in the template:

- Directions: Brief instructions for how to use the template. Be sure to scroll all the way down to see all the directions.
- Draw: This is a 60-column-by-30-row sheet where you can create your pixel art drawing.
- Fractions 8x8: This tab allows you to make a pixel art drawing inside of an 8-by-8-inch grid, and then you determine the fractions represented by each color you used.
- Fractions 10x10: Same as above but with a bigger grid.
- Fractions 12x12: Same as above but with an even bigger grid.
- Area: This tab allows you to make a pixel art drawing and then determine the area in square units, represented by each color you used.

Directions for Creating Pixel Art

Here are the directions for creating pixel art with the template:

1. Click on the tab in the template titled Draw.
2. For your easy reference, the color key will be displayed at the top with each color in the column with its corresponding letter.
3. To color in the cells, simply type in any lower-case letter from a to s and the corresponding color will be applied to the cell.
4. If you want to choose white, just leave the cell blank. Altogether, this gives you twenty colors to choose from.
5. To change the color in a cell, just type in a new letter.
6. To remove the color from a cell, just delete the letter from the cell.
7. To move around to other cells, use the **arrows keys** or your **mouse**.

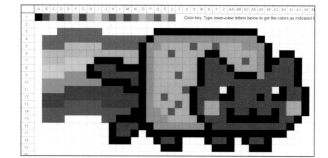

8. To save time, you can select a large set of cells and then copy and paste them into other sections of the sheet.
9. Also, you can click in a cell, then click and drag the little **square handle** in the bottom right corner to drag that cell's color into other cells.
10. Since this is a Google Sheet, don't forget that you can share the Sheet with other people to collaboratively work on the pixel art.

DRAW ACTIVITIES

Pixel art can be used for many educational activities. The Draw tab is a tab for open-ended drawing of whatever pixel art you would like to make. This could be used for many activities, including:

- General creativity: Have students be creative and make whatever they like.
- Art: Have students create their own artistic works, or pixel versions of existing art.
- Tech skills: This so great for younger students to practice typing, using the arrow keys, using the mouse, clicking and dragging, and more.
- Characters: Have students draw characters from a story read in class or for a story the students are writing.
- Concepts: Ask students to illustrate a science concept they are learning.
- Retelling: Have students show an event from history or from a story.
- Mapping: Have students create a map of your neighborhood, state, country, a famous battle, land forms, et cetera.

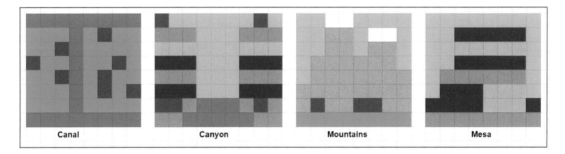

| Canal | Canyon | Mountains | Mesa |

FRACTION ACTIVITIES

In addition to the open-ended activities you can do on the Draw tab, the template contains a few pre-made activity tabs. These lend themselves specifically to math concepts:

1. There are three Fractions tabs. Each tab provides a grid for the student to draw in. The grids are 8 by 8, 10 by 10, and 12 by 12.

2. After creating their drawing inside of the given grid, the student then counts up how many squares of each color they used.

3. These numbers are typed into the boxes on the right of the Sheet to show the fractions each color represents.

4. Next the student can simplify the fractions (if possible) by typing in the reduced version of each fraction to the right of the original fractions.

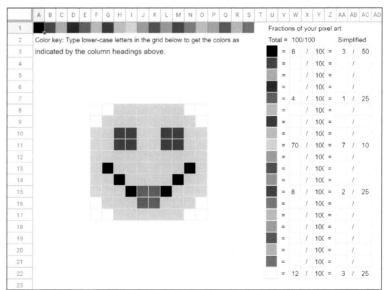

AREA ACTIVITY

- There is one Area tab. The student can create their drawing anywhere in the tab.
- After creating their drawing, the student then counts up how many squares of each color they used.
- These numbers represent the area in square units that color covers.
- These numbers are typed into the boxes on the left of the Sheet to show the areas for each color.

WHEN FINISHED

After completing any of the drawings or activities, there are some options for cleaning up your creation:

- You can delete the color key at the top of the sheet if you would like.
- You can delete any extra rows or columns if you want. Click on the row or column heading, then click **Edit** and choose **Delete row** or **Delete column**.
- You can remove the gridlines if you want by clicking **View** and **unchecking Gridlines**.

You can then share your art in the usual ways through the Share button, as a link, as a PDF, or by printing. Google Sheets does not have an option to export the Sheet as an image, but you can use one of many screen capture tools to take a screenshot of your creation and then save that as an image. One good example would be the Chrome extension Nimbus Screenshot.

To get a good screenshot of your art, do the following:

1. First, follow the same steps as if you are going to print the Sheet by clicking **File**, then **Print**.
2. Adjust the print settings as needed, including the **Scale** option, to get it to look just the way you want.
3. Now that you have a nice clean view of your creation, use the screen-capture tool of your choice to take and save a screenshot.

You can access the following digital resources for this project via the "Book Links" page of my blog:

- Twenty-Color Pixel Art Template, including:
- Draw Activity
- Fraction Activity
- Area Activity

32: MONDRIAN ART ACTIVITY

Though you might not recognize the name, you most likely will recognize the look. Mondrian art is an abstract form of art that uses a creative layout of squares and rectangles, often filled in with primary colors.

This style of painting was popularized by Dutch artist Piet Mondrian in the early twentieth century. In addition to influencing other artists, the Mondrian look has shown up in fashion, architecture, advertising, design, and more.

Because Mondrian art is composed of many different-sized rectangles and squares, it is the perfect match for digital tools. . . specifically, Google Sheets!

Some fun math applications of Mondrian art for your students include the following:

- Area: Find the area in square units for each of the colors used.
- Fractions: Find the fraction that each color represents, and simplify to the lowest form.

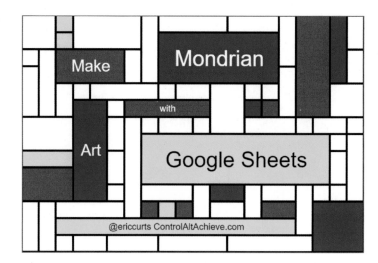

MONDRIAN ART TEMPLATE

To help save some time, I have put together a Mondrian art template in Google Sheets. You can get your own copy of the template on the "Book Links" page of my blog. You certainly do not have to use the template, but it has a few things set up to make the project easier: square cells, thick borders, and primary colors.

SQUARE CELLS

Normally, spreadsheets have rectangular cells that are not square. To make Mondrian art, though, you will want to start with a base of all square cells, which you can then merge as needed to form the rectangles you want. In this template I have changed the column widths and row heights to make all the cells square.

THICK BORDERS

Mondrian art typically has thick black lines between all of the rectangles in the finished work. I have already added these in the template.

PRIMARY COLORS

Mondrian usually filled the rectangles in his paintings with primary colors. Later, when you color your rectangles, you can just use the standard colors provided in the **Fill color** (paint roller) button.

I did include a few custom colors in the template, though, based on actual Mondrian paintings, if you wish to use those.

Next, let's look at how to make your Mondrian art.

MERGE CELLS

As mentioned above, Mondrian art is composed of many rectangles of different sizes. In our template, all of the cells are square, so what we need to do is merge cells together to create our rectangles.

To merge some cells:

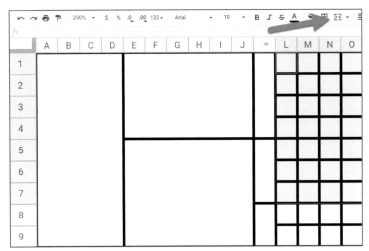

1. Click in a cell that will be one of the corners of your rectangle.
2. Click and hold down your mouse button, and with the mouse button held down, drag to select the other cells that will make up your rectangle.
3. Alternately, if you prefer to use your keyboard, you can click in one cell, then hold down the **Shift** key, then use your **arrow** keys to select more cells.
4. With the desired cells selected, click on the **Merge cells** button in the top toolbar (or click **Format** in the menu bar, and choose **Merge cells** from the drop-down menu).
5. The cells will be merged!

Keep repeating this process to merge cells into rectangles to create your design.

NOTE If needed, you can always unmerge cells as well. Simply click on the merged cells, then click the **Merge cells** button in the toolbar, or click **Format** and then **Merge cells** and then **Unmerge**.

✏ COLOR CELLS

After you have merged some cells, you will want to fill some of the rectangles in with color. In a typical Mondrian piece, the majority of the rectangles will stay white, and you will just fill in colors here and there. Of course, there is no "right" way to make your artwork, as long as it expresses what you wish.

To fill in a rectangle with color:

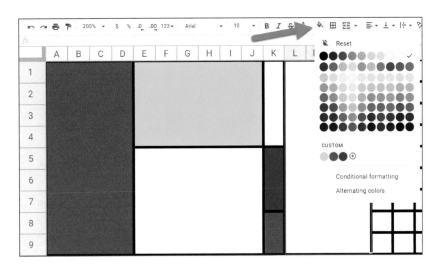

1. Click inside a rectangle to select it.
2. Then click the **Fill color** button in the top toolbar (it looks like a paint roller).
3. You can pick from any color you would like to use to fill in the rectangle.
4. Mondrian typically used primary colors, and our template includes a few custom colors

that closely match the ones he used. Again, there are no "right" colors to use, so be as creative as you wish.

✎ DELETE UNUSED ROWS AND COLUMNS

Chances are you will probably not use all the squares in the template to make your Mondrian Art. If you find you have extra rows and columns that you do not need, you can delete these extras so that just your artwork if left. To delete rows or columns, do the following:

1. Use your mouse to select the rows or columns you want to delete. To do so, click and drag over the columns or row headers.
2. With the columns or rows selected, right-click on the headers and choose **Delete columns** or **Delete rows**.
3. Alternately, you can click **Edit** in the top menu bar and then select **Delete columns** or **Delete rows**.

✎ SHARE YOUR CREATION

When your Mondrian art is finally done, you will want to share your creation with others. This could be done as usual by sharing the Sheet, as a link, as a PDF, as a screen-shot, or by printing.

RESOURCES

You can access the following digital resource for this project via the "Book Links" page of my blog:

• Mondrian Art Template

33: RANDOM WRITING PROMPT GENERATOR

When our students set out to write a poem or story, a blank page can be both exciting (so much potential!) and intimidating (where do you begin?).

One way to help inspire our students' imaginations is to provide them with writing prompts. This can help them think of new ideas, jog their memories, make a connection, or simply inspire them to try out a topic. But where can they get writing prompts?

Certainly there are loads of helpful websites providing multitudes of prompts. Another option, though, is to use a Google Sheet. Yes, that's right. A Google Sheet (often thought of as just a math tool) can help inspire writing!

I have used Google Sheets to create a Random Writing Prompt Generator that randomly pulls from a list of about two thousand adjectives and one thousand nouns to create over two million unique prompts. This is available on the "Book Links" page of my blog. See below to learn how it works, and get more ideas on how to help your students make poems, stories, or other creations.

✎ The Template

The Random Writing Prompt Generator has three tabs:

- The Prompts tab: Here you will find twenty randomly generated writing prompts in the form of an adjective followed by a noun. These can be used for the title of a poem or the topic of a story.
- The Adjectives tab: Here you will find a list of about two thousand adjectives.
- The Nouns tab: Here you will find a list of about one thousand nouns.

To get a new set of *twenty random prompts*, press the **Ctrl** and **R** keys to force the Sheet to recalculate. Many of the prompts may not make sense or may not be a good match— but students will likely find one or two interesting, funny, or inspiring combinations in the list.

Students should write down any prompts that seem interesting to them, then refresh the page to get a new list of prompts. They can repeat this process until they have a good list of prompts to draw from to begin their writing.

	A	B
1	Below are random phrases to serve as writings prompts. They can be used for the title of a poem or the subject of a story. The prompts are created by randomly combining an adjective with a noun. You can get a new random list of prompts by refreshing the page or pressing "Ctrl" and "R".	
2		
3	highfalutin boat	fabulous calculator
4	major arithmetic	required rainstorm
5	frilly tooth	adept dirt
6	far-off kiwi	ridiculous plate
7	finicky writing	busy shadow
8	rainy muscle	winged rail
9	thankful alien	slimy goat
10	graceful writer	perky size
11	active boat	petty cow
12	opulent picture	floppy nuggets
13		

If you want to change the word banks, you can edit the Adjectives or Nouns tabs:

- **Delete** any row to remove a word.
- **Add** more rows at the bottom to add your own words.
- The formula on the **Prompts** tab will pull from your new list of available words.

✎ Nerdy Stuff

For those interested in how the Sheet works, the formula I wrote to randomly generate the prompts is:

=INDIRECT("Adjectives!A"&RANDBETWEEN(1,COUNTA(Adjectives!A:A)))&" "&
INDIRECT("Nouns!A"&RANDBETWEEN(1,COUNTA(Nouns!A:A)))

Here is how it basically works:

- The Adjectives tab contains a list of adjectives and the Nouns tab contains a list of nouns.
- I use the COUNTA function to determine how many adjectives and nouns are available in their respective tabs (in case someone wants to remove any words or add new ones).
- I use the RANDBETWEEN function to randomly choose one of the rows from the Adjectives tab and one from the Nouns tab.

- I then use the "&" operator to join the two words together with a space in between, generating the final writing prompt.

✏ Sample Poems

And in the spirit of sharing, available via the "Book Links" page of my blog are several poems I have written using randomly generated titles. This is something I have done for years with my children as a fun family activity. You will find links to these poems:

- "Moonstruck Conifer"
- "Elemental Love"
- "Invisible Poodle"
- "Fallen Vowel"
- "Smallest Pony"
- "Squirming Curtain"

You can access the following digital resources for this project via the "Book Links" page of my blog:

- Random Writing Prompt Generator
- Sample poems

34: Emoji Writing Prompt Generator

In the last chapter we looked at a Google Sheets Random Writing Prompt Generator, which randomly combined nouns and adjectives to give students inspiration for writing projects. In this chapter we are going to take a twist on that idea... with emojis!

They say a picture is worth a thousand words. If that is so, emojis should be able to carry even more meaning and ideas and inspiration than just words.

There are several great reasons for using emojis as writing prompts:

- Since emojis are images, they can be used with students of any age, language, or reading ability.
- They can provide a wide range of ideas—each student will have their own interpretations of the pictures.
- Emojis are very popular with students, so they will likely have familiarity with the images.
- They are fun! And writing should be fun. And learning should be fun. And school should be fun!
- Getting started with writing can often be a challenge for our students (or anyone for that matter). Using emojis to generate ideas can be a fun and effective way to help students create stories, no matter how big or how small. In other words:

✎ The Template

To create an emoji writing prompt generator, I used Google Sheets. Though we usually think of a spreadsheet as containing numbers, Google Sheets actually supports images, including all the standard emojis. I have created an Emoji Random Writing Prompt Generator, which is available on the "Book Links" page of my blog.

The Emoji Random Writing Prompt Generator spreadsheet has six tabs along the bottom:

- Directions tab: Here you will find the directions for using the spreadsheet.
- 2 Emojis tab: This tab randomly generates two emojis as a writing prompt.
- 3 Emojis tab: This tab randomly generates three emojis as a writing prompt.
- 4 Emojis tab: This tab randomly generates four emojis as a writing prompt.
- 5 Emojis tab: This tab randomly generates five emojis as a writing prompt.
- Data tab: This tab has a set of more than eight hundred emojis, from which the other tabs randomly pull.

To view the writing prompts, students can click their selected tabs at the bottom of the spreadsheet, depending on how many emojis they want to use. If they do not find inspiration in the emojis they get, they can easily generate new random combinations as follows:

- Press the **Ctrl** and **R** keys to force the Sheet to "recalculate," which will pull up new random emojis.
- Simply **reload** the Sheet in the browser.

When a student finds a set of emojis that works for them, they can use them as inspiration for their writing—for example, they can include each of the items or ideas associated with the emojis somewhere in their story or poem.

You may also want to have the students indicate somewhere in their document which emojis they used. If they want to, they can even copy and paste the emoji images straight from the spreadsheet into their Google Doc.

If you want to edit the available emojis, you can make changes to the Data tab. Depending on the age and needs of your students, you may want to delete some of the rows from that tab to remove those emojis as options.

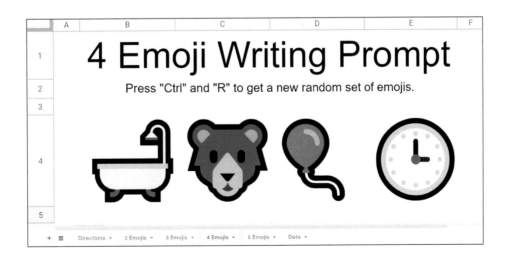

✎ Nerdy Stuff

For those interested in how the random emoji generator works, here is the formula I use:

=CHAR(INDIRECT("Data!B"&RANDBETWEEN(1,COUNTA(Data!B:B))))

Here's how it works:

- The Data tab contains the standard character codes for the emojis I chose to include, one code per row.
- I use the COUNTA function to determine how many emoji codes are available in the Data tab (in case someone chooses to remove some of the emojis from their copy).
- I use the RANDBETWEEN function to randomly choose one of the rows from the Data tab.
- I input the randomly chosen character code into the CHAR function, which then displays the corresponding emoji image.

You can access the following digital resource for this project via the "Book Links" page of my blog:

- Emoji Random Writing Prompt Generator

35: Educational Games and Activities with Flippity

Educational games can be a fun way to engage students while also teaching or reviewing subject area content. They can include activities such as word searches, crossword puzzles, bingo games, flashcards, *Jeopardy!* games, and more.

There are lots of tools online that can be used to create such activities. One creative option is to use Google Sheets templates from Flippity. Flippity is a free website that provides a wide range of templates that you can download, fill in with your own content, and then play online.

As an educator you can make these activities for your own use, or for review games for your class. Students can also use Flippity to make their own activities, which could be a fun alternative project for those interested. For example, a student could create a set of digital flash cards for the content being covered in a particular unit.

See below for how to access the templates and then use them to make your own interactive projects.

 Flippity Activities

Begin by going to the Flippity website at flippity.net.

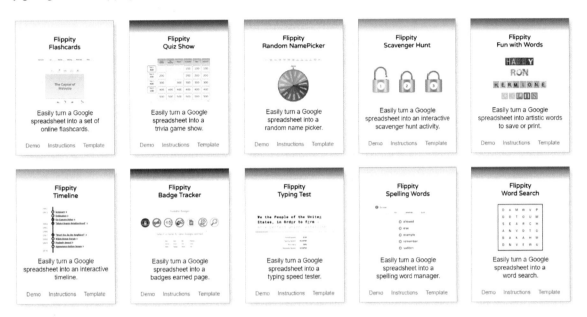

There you will see a grid of thumbnails showing the wide variety of interactive games and activities you can create with Flippity. New ones are added from time to time, but as of this writing, the following templates are available:

- Flashcards: Add text, images, and videos to create a flash card set.
- Quiz Show: Play the Flippity version of a *Jeopardy!* game.
- Random Name Picker: Use for selecting a random student or creating random groups and teams.
- Scavenger Hunt: Create your own *Breakout*-style game.
- Fun With Words: Make artistic versions of words.
- Timeline: Create an interactive time line.
- Badge Tracker: Display digital badges earned by students.
- Typing Test: Practice typing speed and accuracy with custom texts.
- Spelling Words: Create spelling lists for students to practice with a variety of games.
- Word Search: Make an interactive word search.
- Crossword Puzzle: Generate a crossword puzzle from words and clues.
- Word Scramble: Make word scramble puzzles from a list of words, including a final phrase to solve.
- Bingo: Play online or using printouts.
- Hangman: Play five styles of hangman from a custom word list.
- Progress Indicator: Track and display student progress, such as pages read.
- Matching Game: Create a memory game with words and/or pictures.
- Mad Libs: Make a story for users to fill in with different parts of speech.
- Mix and Match: Randomly combine words or phrases to make writing prompts.
- Tournament Bracket: Generate a bracket from a list of four to sixty-four competitors.
- Certificate Quiz: Make a self-grading quiz that generates a certificate when completed.

If you would like to try out an activity or game to see how it works, simply click the **Demo** link below the thumbnail. This will open the activity loaded with demo content you can test.

If you would like to learn even more about an activity, click the **Instructions** link to get a page with detailed information about that activity.

 # MAKE A COPY OF A TEMPLATE

Once you have selected the activity you want to create, you will need to make a copy of its Google Sheets template:

1. Click the **Template** link at the bottom of the thumbnail for an activity.
2. You will get a new window asking if you would like a copy of the Sheet.
3. Click **Make a copy** and the copy will be created.
4. When you are done, you will have your own copy of the template with demo content entered.

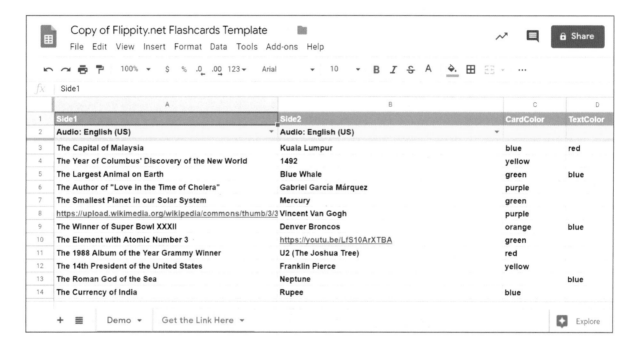

 # FILL IN YOUR CONTENT

Now that you have a copy of the Google Sheets template for your activity, you will want to remove the placeholder content and insert your own:

1. Delete the existing content in the template.
2. Be careful *not* to edit any cells with a blue background, as those cells are needed for Flippity to function properly.
3. Now add in your own text, such as clues and answers for the activity.
4. Some templates support links to images and YouTube videos.

PUBLISH THE SPREADSHEET

Once you have entered your content into the template, there is another step before you can play the game or run the activity. At the moment, your Sheet is private just to you, so Flippity is not able to access your content. You need to publish the Sheet for Flippity to be able to use it:

1. Click **File**, then click **Publish to the Web**.
2. When the pop-up window opens, click **Publish**.
3. Click **OK** when asked if you are sure.
4. You can close out of the pop-up window after publishing.

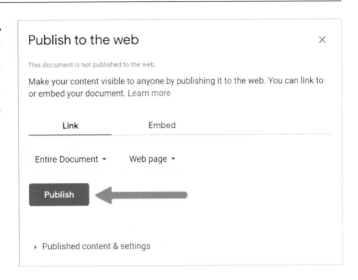

GET THE LINK FOR THE ACTIVITY

You are now ready to try out your game or activity! To do so:

1. Look at the bottom of the Sheet to find the table titled **Get the Link Here**.
2. On this Sheet you will find the link to run the interactive Flippity activity with your content.
3. Click the link to open and run the activity.
4. You can also copy the link and make it available to others so that they can run the activity as well.

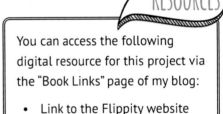

RESOURCES

You can access the following digital resource for this project via the "Book Links" page of my blog:

- Link to the Flippity website

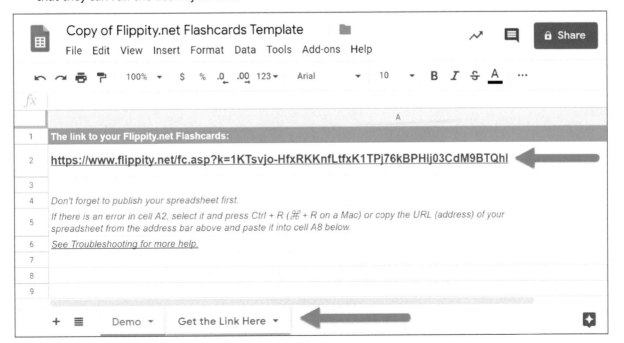

36: Rebooting You: KISS and Tech Up

When it comes to technology integration, we are often encouraged to think outside the box, transform education, revolutionize the learning process, and aim for the stars. As noble and well-meaning as all this is, sometimes it can have the unintended consequence of impeding the growth of educational technology in schools.

How is that possible?

A while back I had the privilege of working with several teachers over many months on technology integration projects. The plan was to explore SAMR, the Four Cs, ISTE Standards, and technology tools. Then they would create a technology-integrated activity for their students.

As we approached the time when participants would develop and deliver the lesson, I heard variations of the same concern from many of the teachers:

- Is my project big enough?
- Am I using enough technology tools?
- Does this really revolutionize teaching and learning?

The teachers were stressing out that their lessons may not be awesome enough to count as real technology integration. They felt intimidated and unsure and reluctant to move forward.

Seeing the problem, I tried to reassure them that they were fine. They just needed to embrace the philosophy of KISS. No, not the makeup-wearing rock band. What I mean is the phrase "Keep it simple, stupid" (or "sweetie," if you prefer to be nicer).

 ## KISS

When it comes to technology integration, certainly we do want to aim high. We need to prepare our students with the skills they need for their futures. These can encompass the Four Cs (Communication, Collaboration, Creativity, and Critical Thinking), the ISTE Standards for students, the P21 Framework, and higher levels of SAMR.

Yes, we need to have high goals—but we can't reach them is one giant leap. Often, the best way to meet our big goals in to take small steps toward them. We need to balance best practices with being practical.

Rather than creating a massive, earth-shattering, multi-technology lesson, I encouraged the teachers to simply take a lesson they have done in the past and *tweak it*. Find a way to introduce technology into the old lesson

to improve it a bit. Maybe check off one of the Four Cs. Perhaps bump up one step in the SAMR model.

In short . . . to KISS.

When integrating technology, there are several good reasons to take small steps and keep it simple, which I talk about below.

1) Repetition

Let's say you do go all out and create the Technology Lesson to End All Lessons. It uses five different technology tools, spans several weeks, and checks off all six strands of the ISTE Standards. When the project ends and the dust settles you will pat yourself on the back, look at all you have accomplished, and proclaim "I am never going to do that again!"

It's just not realistic. If integrating technology is that much work, you may do it once for a graduate class requirement, but you can't do the same thing week after week.

Instead, if you make a small, but meaningful change with technology, you will be much more likely to try it again with a future lesson. Steps, not leaps, in the right direction are something you can repeat, and will want to repeat and grow from.

2) Replication

Not only will you want to repeat your use of technology, but your colleagues will be inspired to do the same. They may not be, though, if the lesson is too big and unwieldy.

If you do create that massive technology integration project, other teachers in your school may be impressed by you, but they will not be encouraged by you. They might think:

- Sure, that works for Eric. He is a technology geek.
- Or: Sure, Eric can do that. His students have access to Chromebooks all the time.
- Or: Okay, Eric can pull that off. He doesn't have a life, so he has time to make that work.

Instead, if you show your co-workers that neat one-period activity, or that cool way students used that one Web app, or the way you tweaked an old lesson to let kids collaborate, they will say, "Cool, I can do that. That looks easy."

3) Reinforcement

Finally, when we take small steps with technology, we tend to focus on its real point: supporting teaching and learning. If your goal is to help students learn, you will find ways for technology to come alongside naturally to reinforce the content and skills being taught.

On the other hand, if your goal is to devise a technology-rich lesson, you may focus more on the technology than the learning. The learning always needs to drive the technology, not the other way around.

When properly integrated, technology essentially becomes invisible. Sure, it is there the whole time, but it is there to support learning, help students collaborate, encourage communication, foster creativity, and spark critical thinking. When we keep it simple, we focus on learning, and find ways for technology to make learning better.

Conclusion

So, as you look for ways to use technology in your classroom, remember to keep it simple. Yes, you absolutely need to aim high, strive to transform learning, and plan to change the world. Just do it one step at a time. Just KISS and tech up.

ACKNOWLEDGMENTS

This book would not be possible without the support and encouragement of so many people:

- Thank you to the educators everywhere who have read, used, and inspired the posts and activities on my *Control Alt Achieve* blog.
- Thank you to Dave and Shelley Burgess for believing in me and the potential for this book to impact teachers and students.
- Thank you to the Reading List for their expert guidance in the editing and preparation of this book.
- Thank you to North Canton City Schools and SPARCC/Stark County Educational Service Center for giving me the opportunity to teach and learn with such amazing educators.
- Thank you to Google for Education for creating and providing such powerful tools for schools everywhere and for your commitment to education.

ABOUT THE AUTHOR

Eric has been in education for twenty-eight years. He started out as a math teacher and became a technology specialist for North Canton City Schools. He currently serves as a technology integration specialist for SPARCC in Canton, Ohio, where he supports educators in using technology for teaching and learning. This includes implementation, training, and support for G Suite for Education tools and other technology initiatives.

In addition to being a G Suite Certified Trainer and Innovator, Eric serves as the co-leader for GEG-Ohio, the Google Educator Group of Ohio. This includes hosting a monthly online meeting covering everything new in G Suite from the previous month, as well as championing resources and best practices for using Google tools in schools.

For many years Eric has shared all of his technology resources on his *Control Alt Achieve* blog. The site includes hundreds of blog posts, as well as training videos, help guides, templates, and podcast episodes. The resources focus on creative ways for educators to use technology, and especially Google tools, in the classroom for student learning, creativity, collaboration, and more.

In addition, Eric has traveled the country for more than twenty years providing training for school districts from coast to coast, as well as keynotes and conference sessions at events including ISTE, FETC, TCEA, OETC, and many others.

Outside of educational technology, Eric spends his time with his two beautiful grandchildren, as well as hiking, biking, orienteering, tabletop gaming, cooking, and writing on topics including emotional and mental health and well-being.

MORE FROM

DAVE BURGESS
Consulting, Inc.

Since 2012, DBCI has been publishing books that inspire and equip educators to be their best. For more information on our titles or to purchase bulk orders for your school, district, or book study, visit **DaveBurgessConsulting.com/DBCIbooks**.

MORE TECHNOLOGY & TOOLS

50 Things You Can Do with Google Classroom by Alice Keeler and Libbi Miller

50 Things to Go Further with Google Classroom by Alice Keeler and Libbi Miller

140 Twitter Tips for Educators by Brad Currie, Billy Krakower, and Scott Rocco

Block Breaker by Brian Aspinall

Code Breaker by Brian Aspinall

Google Apps for Littles by Christine Pinto and Alice Keeler

Master the Media by Julie Smith

Reality Bytes by Christine Lion-Bailey, Jesse Lubinsky, Micah Shippee, PhD

Shake Up Learning by Kasey Bell

Social LEADia by Jennifer Casa-Todd

Teaching Math with Google Apps by Alice Keeler and Diana Herrington

Teachingland by Amanda Fox and Mary Ellen Weeks

LIKE A PIRATE™ SERIES

Teach Like a PIRATE by Dave Burgess

eXPlore Like a Pirate by Michael Matera

Learn Like a Pirate by Paul Solarz

Play Like a Pirate by Quinn Rollins

Run Like a Pirate by Adam Welcome

LEAD LIKE A PIRATE™ SERIES

Lead Like a PIRATE by Shelley Burgess and Beth Houf

Balance Like a Pirate by Jessica Cabeen, Jessica Johnson, and Sarah Johnson

Lead beyond Your Title by Nili Bartley

Lead with Appreciation by Amber Teamann and Melinda Miller

Lead with Culture by Jay Billy

Lead with Instructional Rounds by Vicki Wilson

Lead with Literacy by Mandy Ellis

LEADERSHIP & SCHOOL CULTURE

Culturize by Jimmy Casas

Escaping the School Leader's Dunk Tank by Rebecca Coda and Rick Jetter

From Teacher to Leader by Starr Sackstein

The Innovator's Mindset by George Couros

It's OK to Say "They" by Christy Whittlesey

Kids Deserve It! by Todd Nesloney and Adam Welcome

Live Your Excellence by Jimmy Casas

Let Them Speak by Rebecca Coda and Rick Jetter

The Limitless School by Abe Hege and Adam Dovico

Next-Level Teaching by Jonathan Alsheimer

The Pepper Effect by Sean Gaillard

The Principled Principal by Jeffrey Zoul and Anthony McConnell

Relentless by Hamish Brewer

The Secret Solution by Todd Whitaker, Sam Miller, and Ryan Donlan

Start. Right. Now. by Todd Whitaker, Jeffrey Zoul, and Jimmy Casas

Stop. Right. Now. by Jimmy Casas and Jeffrey Zoul

They Call Me "Mr. De" by Frank DeAngelis

Unmapped Potential by Julie Hasson and Missy Lennard

Word Shift by Joy Kirr

Your School Rocks by Ryan McLane and Eric Lowe

Teaching Methods & Materials

All 4s and 5s by Andrew Sharos

Boredom Busters by Katie Powell

The Classroom Chef by John Stevens and Matt Vaudrey

The Collaborative Classroom by Trevor Muir

Copyrighteous by Diana Gill

Ditch That Homework by Matt Miller and Alice Keeler

Ditch That Textbook by Matt Miller

Don't Ditch That Tech by Matt Miller, Nate Ridgway, and Angelia Ridgway

EDrenaline Rush by John Meehan

Educated by Design by Michael Cohen, The Tech Rabbi

The EduProtocol Field Guide by Marlena Hebern and Jon Corippo

The EduProtocol Field Guide: Book 2 by Marlena Hebern and Jon Corippo

Instant Relevance by Denis Sheeran

LAUNCH by John Spencer and A.J. Juliani

Make Learning MAGICAL by Tisha Richmond

Pure Genius by Don Wettrick

The Revolution by Darren Ellwein and Derek McCoy

Shift This! by Joy Kirr

Skyrocket Your Teacher Coaching by Michael Cary Sonbert

Spark Learning by Ramsey Musallam

Sparks in the Dark by Travis Crowder and Todd Nesloney

Table Talk Math by John Stevens

The Wild Card by Hope and Wade King

The Writing on the Classroom Wall by Steve Wyborney

Inspiration, Professional Growth & Personal Development

Be REAL by Tara Martin

Be the One for Kids by Ryan Sheehy

The Coach ADVenture by Amy Illingworth

Creatively Productive by Lisa Johnson

Educational Eye Exam by Alicia Ray

The EduNinja Mindset by Jennifer Burdis

Empower Our Girls by Lynmara Colón and Adam Welcome

Finding Lifelines by Andrew Grieve and Andrew Sharos

The Four O'Clock Faculty by Rich Czyz

How Much Water Do We Have? by Pete and Kris Nunweiler

P Is for Pirate by Dave and Shelley Burgess

A Passion for Kindness by Tamara Letter

The Path to Serendipity by Allyson Apsey

Sanctuaries by Dan Tricarico

The SECRET SAUCE by Rich Czyz

Shattering the Perfect Teacher Myth by Aaron Hogan

Stories from Webb by Todd Nesloney

Talk to Me by Kim Bearden

Teach Better by Chad Ostrowski, Tiffany Ott, Rae Hughart, and Jeff Gargas

Teach Me, Teacher by Jacob Chastain

TeamMakers by Laura Robb and Evan Robb

Through the Lens of Serendipity by Allyson Apsey

The Zen Teacher by Dan Tricarico

Children's Books

Beyond Us by Aaron Polansky

Cannonball In by Tara Martin

Dolphins in Trees by Aaron Polansky

I Want to Be a Lot by Ashley Savage

The Princes of Serendip by Allyson Apsey

The Wild Card Kids by Hope and Wade King

Zom-Be a Design Thinker by Amanda Fox

Made in the USA
Columbia, SC
26 May 2020